"This book is sure to be the go-to resource for LGBT- is an extraordinary educator and anyone reading this ~~book is sure to expe~~ Kryss' passion for inclusion. Kryss is one of the greatest allies to the LGBT+ community I've ever met; she is a dear friend and truly one of a kind. I know that readers will learn more from this book than from any other existing resource and I emphatically support this book!"

—Jazz Jennings, transgender icon, multi-award
winner, and star of TLC's I Am Jazz

"Kryss Shane has created an invaluable resource for any school administrator, curriculum expert, or advocate who wants to make sure that schools are affirming of sexual and gender diversity. For many years, the mental health and education professionals have sounded the alarm bell about the role of schools in LGBTQ+ suicide risk. We know that LGBTQ+ youth experience harassment by peers and teachers, physical and sexual assault because of perceived sexual orientation or gender identity, and have thoughts of suicide and make suicide attempts 2–7x as often as cisgender heterosexual students. The 'safe schools' movement is not enough. We must highlight the beautiful life that queer kids can have and that is exactly what Kryss Shane has done with her book. She has provided foundational information about LGBTQ+ youth and how schools can integrate affirming content into their curriculum and school environment. Not a moment too soon."

—Dr Jonathan Singer, President of the
American Association of Suicidology

"In my decades-long journey as an advocate and policy-maker promoting diversity, inclusion, fairness, and equality, Kryss Shane shines among—and often above—the most dedicated, sincere, seasoned, and effective leaders in the field. This publication could not be more timely. If you are an advocate, an educator, a parent, a co-worker, friend, or neighbor to an LGBT+ identified youth, Kryss is the most engaging go-to coach and educator on best practices for creating safe and supportive spaces for including LGBT+ youth that are thoughtful, humane, and encouraging to all committed to the idea that all youth have a right to a solid, safe, and healthy and compassionate community. What Kryss provides in these pages is the interactive coaching and guidelines that many educators have been waiting for to help create and advance that kind of environment where all youth can thrive."

—Andrea Shorter, Co-Founder of Bayard Rustin LGBT Coalition, former
Director of Community Relations, Out & Equal Workplace Advocates,
former Director of Marriage Equality and Coalitions Strategies, Equality
California, 2009 David Bohnett Gay and Lesbian Leadership Fellow,
Inclusive and Safe Community Building consultant and strategist

"All parents want their children to attend a school that is safe and treats them with respect, regardless of their child's race, sex, national origin, religion, gender, or sexual orientation. An inclusive approach will improve the learning environment, help all children succeed, and make our schools stronger and safer."

—Mary Jo Kilroy, former Member of Congress (CD-OH-15) and Member of the Congressional LGBT Equality Caucus. As a Member of Congress, she was a co-sponsor of the Matthew Shepard and James Byrd Jr. Hate Crimes Prevention Act. As a Columbus School Board Member, she authored the first anti-harassment policies on the basis of race, sex, and sexual orientation, and training on the issues facing LGBT+ students for teachers, counselors, nurses, and principals

"Creating LGBT+ inclusive curricula and inclusive school spaces is not only best practice, it is also consistent with a school's legal obligations to provide a safe and welcoming learning environment for all students. This book provides this information to administrators and educators in a thorough and easily accessible manner and is vital to ensuring that all students, including LGBT+ students, have equal educational opportunity."

—Asaf Orr, Esq. Senior Staff Attorney and Transgender Youth Project Director, National Center for Lesbian Rights

"When schools are not LGBT+ inclusive, it's telling our children—our future— that they are not worthy of love and acceptance for who they are or of even *being* here. Being inclusive is not difficult and it literally saves our children's lives. Ms. Shane's vast expertise and experience with the LGBT+ population provides a golden opportunity for schools to learn properly the first time around and avoid detrimental mistakes as they train staff and create inclusive policies."

—Kathryn and Jeremy Mathis, victorious litigants in the landmark 2013 case in which the Colorado Civil Rights Division ruled in favor of their then 6-year-old transgender child to use the girls' bathroom at her elementary school in Colorado

"LGBTQ activism has been a part of our nations for generations and as we continue to gain rights there are movements that work to take away and deny rights for LGBTQ people. *The Educator's Guide to LGBT+ Inclusion* is vital because having our history taught in schools will help to elevate acceptance and equality."

—Marti Gould Cummings, New York City Council Candidate (Manhattan's District 7), Luminary Award Winner for Dedication to Homeless LGBTQ Youth and listed on the 2018 Out 100 list for Out *magazine*

"School educators and staff, bolstered by thoughtful, sensitive policies and training that embraces diversity via *The Educator's Guide to LGBT+ Inclusion,* can create a protective, inclusive, and growth-producing environment for LGBT+ youth. Kryss Shane brings a near-lifelong passion as an ally, along with her social worker's ability to bear witness to human struggles and identify solutions to her writing."

—Susan Mankita, LCSW, Florida International University educator, NASW Pioneer, and 2019 NASW-FL President

"LGBT+ inclusivity and education in schools is extremely important, not only for children, but for their families and home environments as well. Through *The Educator's Guide to LGBT+ Inclusion,* children can learn and be exposed to issues concerning the LGBT+ community in a setting that is open, honest/ accurate, and sensitive."

—James Valletti, theatrical director and producer including off-Broadway's Tales from the Tunnel *and many other Broadway and off-Broadway works*

"We send our children to school for an education, but 'education' reaches far beyond the three R's. Social development can often eclipse academic achievement in both positive and negative ways. *The Educator's Guide to LGBT+ Inclusion* provides these vital components. Kryss Shane has dedicated her life to fostering the equality of LGBTQ people. Would that we all could have that kind of empathy with our fellow humans."

—Fredi Walker-Browne, actress, writer, director; creator of The Professional Skills for Actors Series™ *and founder of Big Spoon Productions, as well as Joanne in the original Broadway company of* Rent

"From the start in her life, Kryss has demonstrated a deep caring of all people, but especially those at risk, the LGBTQ community. Through reading *The Educator's Guide to LGBT+ Inclusion,* every reader will experience her love of all people and working hard to expand the minds of those confused by LGBT+ students' needs."

—Melissa Canaday, television, film, and theater actor, charity fundraiser; wife and mother to television, film, and Broadway actors, aunt to Trevor Canaday

"*The Educator's Guide to LGBT+ Inclusion* is a must-read for all education professionals because the purpose of school is to help prepare students to function in the world and LGBT+ people are a valuable part of the functioning world. Her over 23 years' training and multiple degrees makes Kryss Shane the perfect person to discuss LGBT+ issues."

—*Richard E. Waits, Broadway actor and creator of his one-man show* Mama Rose

"I strongly believe having an inclusive school environment is essential to normalizing and breaking down the stigmas surrounding LGBTQ+ issues and *The Educator's Guide to LGBT+ Inclusion* is the perfect way to make this happen. Kryss is the right person to train American educators because her significant experience is second to none and she offers guidance in a way that makes everyone feel comfortable."

—*Genevieve Buechner, film and television actress, including* The 100, Caprica, UnREAL, *and* Supernatural

"In these times, when some forces work to tear apart the fabric of our society and our relationships, particularly for those identified as an 'other,' we need informed and effective voices to calm, educate, and unify. Kryss Shane is that voice. *The Educator's Guide to LGBT+ Inclusion* will be a huge asset and driving force for any school that aims to create and support a more inclusive society."

—*Michelan Sisti, 30+ years as a* Muppets *and* Jim Henson's Creature Shop *performer, including Michaelangelo in the* Teenage Mutant Ninja Turtles *films*

"I know that my students can't thrive in my classroom unless they feel safe, supported, and valued. It is my job to create an inclusive classroom community that celebrates diversity. It's important that I use teaching materials students can relate to and see themselves in. My job is to choose words that are inclusive and don't communicate assumptions about gender."

—*Julia Handelman, elementary school teacher and founder of Youth Yoga Project*

"When students and staff are free from fears of bullying or being outed, they are much better equipped to focus and much more receptive to information and for their brain to use that knowledge to be encoded, processed, consolidated (to long-term memory while we sleep), and remembered (able to be retrieved/recalled from said long-term memory). This greatly increases the chances of maximizing their potential."

—*Dr. Bryant Horowitz, neuropsychologist and professor at East Los Angeles College*

The Educator's Guide to
LGBT+ Inclusion

of related interest

How to Transform Your School into an LGBT+ Friendly Place
A Practical Guide for Nursery, Primary and Secondary Teachers
Dr Elly Barnes MBE and Dr Anna Carlile
ISBN 978 1 78592 349 4
eISBN 978 1 78450 684 1

Phoenix Goes to School
A Story to Support Transgender and Gender Diverse Children
Michelle and Phoenix Finch
Illustrated by Sharon Davey
ISBN 978 1 78592 821 5
eISBN 978 1 78450 924 8

**Supporting Transgender and Non-Binary Students
and Staff in Further and Higher Education**
Practical Advice for Colleges and Universities
Dr Matson Lawrence and Dr Stephanie Mckendry
ISBN 978 1 78592 345 6
eISBN 978 1 78450 673 5

Gender Equality in Primary Schools
A Guide for Teachers
Helen Griffin
ISBN 978 1 78592 340 1
eISBN 978 1 78450 661 2

Supporting Gender Diversity in Early Childhood Classrooms
A Practical Guide
*Encian Pastel, Katie Steele, Julie Nicholson, Cyndi Maurer,
Julia Hennock, Jonathan Julian, Tess Unger and Nathanael Flynn*
ISBN 978 1 78592 819 2
eISBN 978 1 78450 914 9

The Educator's Guide to LGBT+ Inclusion

A Practical Resource for K–12 Teachers, Administrators, and School Support Staff

Kryss Shane, MS, MSW, LSW, LMSW (she/her)

Foreword contributed by PostSecret

Afterword by James Lecesne,
Co-founder of The Trevor Project

Jessica Kingsley Publishers
London and Philadelphia

Images on pp.26–29 reproduced with permission of PostSecret.
Image on p.194 reproduced with permission of Morley.

First published in 2020
by Jessica Kingsley Publishers
73 Collier Street
London N1 9BE, UK
and
400 Market Street, Suite 400
Philadelphia, PA 19106, USA

www.jkp.com

Copyright © Kryss Shane 2020
Afterword copyright © James Lecesne 2020

Front cover image source: iStockphoto®.

Library of Congress Cataloging in Publication Data
A CIP catalog record for this book is available from the Library of Congress

British Library Cataloguing in Publication Data
A CIP catalogue record for this book is available from the British Library

ISBN 978 1 78775 108 8
eISBN 978 1 78775 109 5

Printed and bound in the United States

This book is for every educator who comes in early, who leaves late, and whose personal life includes thoughts about their students because a passion for educating doesn't end when the bell rings.

It is for every student, parent, and school staff member who worries about whether their identity will distract from the learning process and whether it is safe to live openly.

This book is for my homelands: small town (the Nordonia community) and big city (Columbus) Ohio, New York City, Miami, and LA. In each, I have studied and learned about the culture, the school systems, and the needs of LGBT+ people. This book was written with these variances in mind, as it is intended to be inclusive to all people, to all schools, in all places.

It is for the activists who risk their safety and their jobs by speaking up in favor of inclusive and supportive policies. This book is for the youth who choose to sit next to the LGBT+ kid sitting alone in the lunchroom because kindness and compassion surpass gender and sexual identities.

This book is for the Matthew Shepards, the Leelah Alcorns, the Jazz Jenningses, the Coy Mathises, for all of their parents, for all of their siblings, and for the ones lucky enough to walk easier through the path of education because of those who have walked it first.

Perhaps, most of all, this book is for the trailblazers who know they are superheroes and for the trailblazers of future "generderations" who have yet to identify their superhero potential. I see you, you matter, and thank heavens you're here and that you're you!

(Note: This manuscript was submitted to the publishing house on June 28, 2019. This was intentionally done to honor further and celebrate the risks and sacrifices of Marsha P. Johnson, Sylvia Rivera, and all who refused to tolerate any more bigotry against the LGBT+ community, thus starting the Stonewall Riots on June 28, 1969. I stand with you, I stand in your shoes, and I will forever stand up for what we all believe(d) in: LGBT+ equality for all.)

Contents

Acknowledgments

When I was four years old, I put "write a book" on my life goals list. That four-year-old (and all the incarnations and transformations of her that followed) fought through so, so much to get from there to here, and I must begin by acknowledging and thanking her for never giving up. I honor her and I hope that she inspires the dreams and goals of the readers and subjects of this book to continue to fight and persevere to reach their goals too, even when they seem too far off to ever happen.

Thank you to my tribe (past and present), individuals who have consistently chosen to prioritize our relationship, no matter the miles, no matter the circumstances, making me feel seen, heard, and validated (alphabetically by first name): Alaina Dobos, Andrea Shorter, Annette Cacao, Ashley Kate Adams, Brian Denny, Bryant Horowitz, Cara (Morton) Burden, Cheryl Kaiser, Chris Andexler, Clarissa Piquero Kierner, Dan Coleman, David Glaubach, Deb Unger, Dimitri Moise, Heather Candela, James Monroe Iglehart, Janet Sasso, Jason (Bacon) Owen, Jason Topel, Jordan Hedeby, Julia Osen Averill, Kara (McElvenny) Crowley, Karen Uslin, Karen Zgoda, Kathy Blazer, Kurt Broz, Lauren Banyar Reich, Leanne Marshall, Lee Watkins, Louise Owen, Matt Deyling, Melvin Abston, Mika Kaneshiro, Rachel Porcellio, Richard E. Waits, Sarah Bellett, Shaun Earl, and Toby Rogers.

Thank you to the other 2/3 of "Team TieDye," Jeanette and Jazz, who fed me pizza and encouragement while making sure that I always had enough tie dye, no matter how focused I was on writing this book, too often to the exclusion of self-care.

Thank you to the K–12 educators and administrators in my life, past and present (alphabetically by first name): Dave Aberth, Dawn Soukup, Deborah Wallace, Jessica Hardt Horowitz, Joe Crowley, Kara (McElvenny) Crowley, Kathy Goodson, Rachel Porcellio, Rich Cinquepalmi, and Ron Ashley.

Thank you to Russ Lottig, who chose (and continues to choose) to parent me even when it was almost impossibly difficult and even when we differ(ed). Thank you to Christine Lottig, a lifelong educator both in the Cleveland City School system and in modeling what true kindness is. I am who I am largely because one chose to be my dad, and because the other chose to let him. Thank you to my Thanksgiving family, the Weldons/ Corrigans, the Zebers/Spicuzzas, and to our late founder Mike Bonacci, Sr. for bringing us all together. Y'all and our kitchen are forever my home, no matter where I travel in from. You have found me when I've been lost, you have broken bread with me, and you have given me a foundation and a consistency that grounds my spirit and nourishes my soul.

Thank you to Susan Mankita, Les Oppenheim, and Benjamin Oppenheim. Thank you to Dr Ken Sinervo and the staff at Center for Endometriosis Care. Thank you to Nikko, to Saba, and to GirlKitty. You have all fixed me, healed me, and contributed to my growth in ways that have benefitted and enriched me more than I could have ever imagined. You smoothed my rough edges and filled my broken spaces with gold. In short, I am better because of you.

Thank you to Jason Uveges and Troy Diana, incredible men who gave me unconditional support, who were gone far too soon, and who left me with a better sense of self and a stronger sense of purpose. Thank you to John Lottig, the loss of whom kept me from remaining lost.

Thank you to my fellow secret-keeper Frank Warren who understands what it means to carry the weight and the privilege of hearing what no one else does. Thank you to the trailblazing James Lecesne with whom I've long walked parallel. Thank you to Andrew James, Maddy Budd, Karina Maduro, and the entire team at Jessica Kingsley Publishers for their work and guidance throughout the creation, publication, marketing, and success of this book. Thank you to Chris Lundquist at LundquistAudio for your audio brilliance and mastery, allowing the audiobook version of this book to let everyone everywhere listen and learn.

Thank you to Bea and Rue and Betty and Estelle, whose talents on screen gave me Dorothy and Blanche and Rose and Sophia, four women I have loved with every watch and every rewatch of every episode, and eight women I aspire to be as strong as.

This book is to pay tribute to the work of artists who shined lights into my life, teaching me that acceptance and love are the only way: Edgar Guest, Paul Williams, Garth Brooks, and Jonathan Larson. This book is to honor the work of women who kick up dust while creating the paths that so many have the privilege of walking down more easily, including Ruth Bader Ginsburg (with whom I am proud to share a birthday), Harriet Tubman, Dolly Parton, Judge Marilyn Milian, Lorraine Toussaint, Gail Vaz-Oxlade, Judith Light, Tyne Daly, Sandra Oh, and Viola Davis. It is to celebrate Marsha P. Johnson and Sylvia Rivera, women who spent their lives overcoming the odds whilst changing the landscape of America and the experiences of American women through their unending brilliance, tenacity, and grit.

In summary, this book is the culmination of everything I am, everything I've learned, and everything I believe will make this world a better place. Thank you to those who take the time to read it, who make an effort to internalize the information contained within it, and who make consistent, persistent efforts to support and affirm LGBT+ people, no matter their own sexual and gender identities.

How Big of a
Problem Is This?

Too often, people fear trying to start a conversation or intervene against negativity. This is not because they do not care or because they do not see the value in improving education and knowledge; it is because they fear saying or doing the wrong thing. However, doing and saying nothing implies agreement or consent with anti-LGBT+ behaviors and policies.

What is life currently like for most LGBT+ youth? According to studies from 2017–2019:[1]

- LGBT+ students are twice as likely to be to be bullied, both online and on school property.
- Almost 30 percent had attempted suicide—more than four times the rate for non-LGBT+ students.
- 77 percent of LGBT+ teens report feeling depressed within the past week.
- 95 percent of LGBT+ youth report having trouble sleeping.
- 89 percent of LGBT+ youth of color report that their racial or ethnic group is regarded negatively at school.
- Only 26 percent say they always feel safe at school.

---

1   These statistics include information gathered and verified by the consistent results of surveys and questionnaires completed by American LGBT+ youth via studies through the following organizations: The Trevor Project; Gay, Lesbian and Straight Education Network (GLSEN); Human Rights Campaign (HRC); Gay & Lesbian Alliance Against Defamation (GLAAD); the National LGBTQ Task Force; and the American Government's Youth Risk Behavior Survey.

- Nearly 18 percent of LGBT+ students reported having been raped at some point in their lives—more than three times the rate of non-LGBT+ students.
- About two-thirds of LGBT+ students reported having been sexually harassed (e.g. sexual remarks made, being touched inappropriately) in school in the past year.
- LGBT+ youth are more than twice as likely to stay home from school to avoid violence they feel might befall them on the way there, or on school grounds.
- Only 5 percent say that their school's staff are fully supportive of LGBT+ people.

Now that we see the impact of what happens when silence prevails, it is clear that speaking up is necessary to protect LGBT+ people in school settings. As for knowing what to do, this book will guide you through the process so that you will feel confident in ascertaining problematic situations and policies, knowing who to speak with to make corrections, and knowing how to speak up in support of LGBT+ safety, security, and inclusion in your school setting.

Preface

This book was not created to push a political agenda, to turn current school systems on their heads, or to undermine learning experiences currently being provided throughout America. Instead, this book aims to enlighten the reader and encourage them to consider the ways that small additions or changes to existing lesson plans and school policies may further benefit their students academically, socially, and emotionally.

Your personal beliefs about the lesbian, gay, bisexual, and transgender (LGBT+) community are your own. While I cannot guarantee you won't reconsider them by the time you've completed this book, please know that it is not my goal to focus on those beliefs. In your personal lives, it is, of course, your prerogative to make choices that best align with your personal beliefs. However, this book focuses on choices, behaviors, and actions taken within the school environment while in the role of an educator.

Some question whether the idea of gay students is new. It can seem as if people are constantly inventing new words to identify their sexuality and gender, making it easy to wonder if this is just some silly way that some adolescents are attempting to make themselves seem more exciting and unique. It stands to reason then that these attempts should not lead to any alterations within the school situation. Some believe that even acknowledging any of these terms only feeds an adolescent's desire to create new terms and new words to stand out more and more from their peers. Others question why there seem to be so many transgender people all of a sudden. Many talk about how no one identified as such in past decades or in previous generations. In both situations, the answer is twofold. There were not many opportunities for people to live as openly as they do now, when it is becoming safer in many states and many countries to publicly identify as something other than a society's typical expected identity options.

In addition, technology has also played a part. In past generations, one person may have felt a certain way and thought they were the only one in the whole world with those thoughts and feelings. Now, because of social media, there are additional opportunities for people to publish and self-publish their experiences, and because people are more easily able to connect to those they identify with, that one person no longer feels they are the only one in the world. Instead, they can hop on a computer or use a browser on their smartphone to connect with others in other communities across the globe who are just like them. Often, this experience allows for a significant amount of validation for the individual who previously thought they were all alone and that the lack of peers sharing this experience meant that their feelings must be wrong and this indicated that something must be wrong with them. This resulted in many around the world feeling lonely, lost, broken, and unworthy. It is easy to see how a person with this belief could experience depression and why so many attempted or committed suicide.

As the saying goes, there's safety in numbers. This is true with sexual and gender minorities as well. Now, support groups and friendship groups exist on social media, which bring people together from all over the world who would never have otherwise met but among whom shared feelings and identities exist. Simultaneously, video-sharing platforms allow individuals to document their life experiences and personal journeys, which can bring comfort in better understanding to viewers, regardless of whether they feel validated within their own communities, schools, and families.

This book is not about whether there are gay people, whether transgender people are a "real thing," or whether there should or should not be dozens of terms people use to self-identify their place in the world. The reality is that there are gay people, there are transgender people, and there are people who self-identify using terms that may be unfamiliar to others. This then leads us to consider whether adults should acknowledge these differences, especially if the adult may believe a student is using a word or term solely for attention. Some may even question how anyone should be expected or required to acknowledge these proclaimed differences, as they may remember that not long ago mental health diagnostic manuals considered homosexuality and transgender identity to be mental illnesses. However, every major mental health organization has spoken out in support and acceptance of LGBT+ people for decades, using research and science to buttress their position that sexual orientation and gender identity are a healthy part of who a person is, not a mental health issue that requires fixing.

Now that we've established that LGBT+ people exist and that none of the science-based professional medical and mental health organizations identify these identities as mental illnesses, it is incumbent upon educators to recognize how school staff and administrators impact their students. Whatever your opinions, whatever your beliefs, it is likely universal that everyone who dedicates their career to the lives of children wants those children to be safe and successful. This is the basis of this book. By recognizing ways that LGBT+ students feel unsafe, unwanted, and unworthy of acceptance, educators have the opportunity to work to minimize those experiences, to maximize the situations as learning experiences, and to help society create children who have healthy self-esteem, an awareness and compassion for their peers, and a youthful excitement for the future that they only get to see and experience if they are guided safely through their education in their formative years.

Foreword contributed by PostSecret

Although many books offer a foreword with insights from one person about why the book's topic matters, there was simply no way that any one person could speak on behalf of the estimated two million American LGBT+ youth, their families, and LGBT+ educators. Instead, the author chose to seek out voices that represent these experiences and their stories. What follows is a contribution from PostSecret, with each postcard representing countless individuals with identical or near-identical experiences and stories.

PostSecret is an ongoing community mail art project. In the 15 years since Frank Warren created PostSecret, he has received more than one million secrets, mailed to him from all over the globe. The PostSecret website is the most popular ad-free website in the world, having had more than 900 million views to date. Thousands of secrets have been on tour at museums throughout the world, including at America's Smithsonian Museum.

This project has become such a phenomenon largely because of how one person's secret has been found to be the secret of many. As such, to see the secret of one is to have the opportunity to identify that this one secret speaks for countless others who hold that same secret or that same experience inside of their hearts.

The following secrets have been personally chosen and graciously contributed to this book by Frank Warren, as he continues to support the mental health, suicide prevention, and acceptance of all people through PostSecret, a goal this book shares with the entire PostSecret community of contributors.

I pretend to be straight so that my parents will still LOVE me.

Our family of 5 used to have so much fun together. I have driven a wedge in my family by the way I treat our gay son. At times I treat him with no respect and unloved. I feel like he screwed things up. I must change my feelings & attitude!!

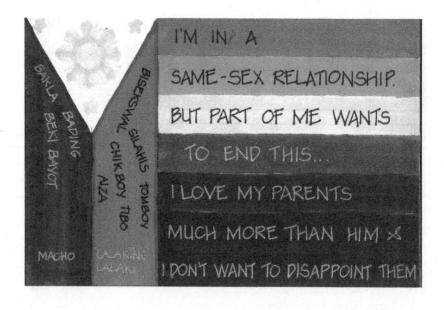

THEY PRANK CALLED ME,
YELLING QUEER AND
FAGGOT THROUGH THE
PHONE. HIGH SCHOOL WAS
THE WORST FOUR YEARS
OF MY LIFE.
I DOUBT they even
remember...

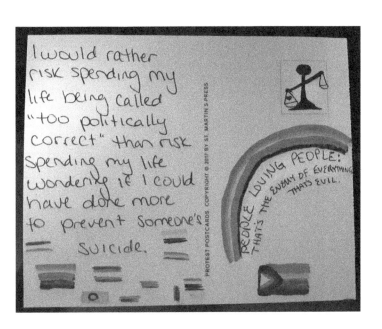

I would rather
risk spending my
life being called
"too politically
correct" than risk
spending my life
wondering if I could
have done more
to prevent someone's
suicide.

PROTEST POSTCARDS COPYRIGHT © 2017 BY ST. MARTIN'S PRESS

PEOPLE LOVING PEOPLE:
THAT'S THE ENEMY OF EVERYTHING
THAT'S EVIL.

Introduction

Before we began this book, let's take a minute to get really real. One of the biggest questions I find most people ask themselves before attending a conference, listening to a speech, or spending time reading a book is *Who cares?* For this reason, I will focus this book only on topics when there is a clear answer, not just to *Who cares?* but also to *Why should I care?*

This isn't because I believe you are incapable of making these connections yourselves, but because I recognize that, by the sheer nature of being an educator, each reader is likely to be significantly overworked and very, very underpaid. In many situations, books that are written for people of a profession are written by people who have never worked within that profession. This results in an entire textbook, reference material, or mandated required reading that works well in theory, but which professionals are swift to acknowledge could never work in practice.

This is why this book will be laid out to make it most accessible for you to find the information you need when you need it, and it will allow you to skip entire chapters if they do not apply to the grade level you teach.

Section I offers foundational knowledge, including terminology and frequently asked questions. This will provide all readers with the opportunity to gain or review information, ensuring that they are up to date in current best practices regarding language and research.

Section II provides scenarios that allow readers to try out what they learned in Section I. Scenarios offer opportunities to think through various real-life school situations. Each scenario is followed by questions to answer as well as guidance so that the readers' answers can be deconstructed, to highlight best practices and to gain further insight into the best ways to meet the needs of the student, student's family, and/or staff member within the scenario. This section can be utilized individually, in small groups, or as a collective. This is a great way to test yourself privately, to collaborate within teaching teams, or to bring a teacher-training seminar together to turn theory into practice!

Section III turns the hypothetical scenarios into real-life action! This section will guide readers in assessing their own school settings, provide scripts to reach out to supervisors to request to discuss making changes in areas where improvements have been identified, and to make alterations within one's own control. This provides the opportunity to discover where your school is successful, gives insights into how to work with your supervisors to make your school more LGBT+ inclusive, and offers methods to improve your own classroom, office, or workplace setting.

The goal of this book is not to make a reader become an expert in this field, but rather to provide foundational knowledge that encompasses the immediate needs of the LGBT+ people within your school system, in a way that causes as little disruption to classrooms and schools as possible. Also, lesson plan ideas within this book are intentionally set *to require little to no preparation time, and little to no expense to purchase supplies or materials*. While a reader is certainly welcome to expand any of the lesson plans provided to be used within more than one class period or to incorporate additional supplies and materials, it is not required.

It is my hope that the information you will read will allow you not just to find implementation opportunities within what you are already teaching, but also that it will help you to understand that the nuances and ways of being mindful of the LGBT+ community can cause benefits to students, staff, family, and the community overall.

The Foundation: Terminology and Insights

Section summary

In this section, you will find foundational information related to the lesbian, gay, bisexual, and transgender communities, as well as to other communities that are under the "sexual orientation and gender identity" umbrella. This includes considerations of safety, allyship, terminology, and frequently asked questions.

How to use this section

This section can be utilized individually or collectively. If you are reading this on your own, consider your current knowledge base and assumptions before each section, then read on and compare your thoughts with the information provided. This will allow you to spend as much or as little time in this section as necessary based on the insight you already have, correcting your misperceptions and filling in knowledge gaps as you read. If you are reading this in a small group setting, please encourage individuals to take time to think independently, then for the groups to share their thoughts with one another. After, the answers from the book can be provided, allowing all participants to compare their thoughts and the group's discussion with the correct answers. If the group is large, breakout groups can be assigned to go through this process in a more manageable way, thus allowing everyone the opportunity to share their thoughts and assumptions as they work through the information in this section.

Section take-away

The purpose of this section is to inform the reader, to correct misunderstandings and outdated knowledge, and to prepare the reader with the foundation necessary to best utilize the entirety of this book.

1

Safety

There are currently no mandates of federal protection and this lack of requirements has too often resulted in no legal consideration for the lesbian, gay, bisexual, transgender (LGBT+) community at all. This means that each state (and sometimes each city within a state) gets to decide whether a person can be discriminated against for being LGBT+. What considerations and protections to provide LGBT+ members of a school community is also left up to specific cities or individual school districts or even individual schools. This can create situations where different schools in the same community may have vastly different rules, policies, and procedures regarding the LGBT+ community. This information is vital to understand so that educators can be mindful of the life experiences of the LGBT+ people with whom they regularly interact.

In some places, there are legal questions and attempts to pass bills to undermine the success of LGBT+ people. These are seen with transgender bathroom bills, with same-sex adoptions, and in situations where a city or state has a clear legal inability to alter a person's gender marker on their identification paperwork. In other areas, specific cities, school districts, or schools may have created their own policies to ensure safety and inclusion of support in the school experience. When looking into LGBT+ people's protections or lack thereof specific to your own community, it is essential to consider not just what has happened within your school or school district, but also what is happening in the surrounding communities.

In some schools, there are signs or stickers identifying a school or classroom as a "safe school." This program has been around for quite some time. The thought behind this, and its goal, is to identify which places and people do not allow homophobic, biphobic, or transphobic language or attacks. When coming out and being out were much rarer, it made sense for the goal to be rooted in recognizing where somebody would not have to hear horrible slurs. In more recent times, however, this is not enough. Now, the most inclusive and welcoming identification is that of being a brave space: a brave-space classroom, or a brave-space office.

This may simply seem to be a change in semantics, but it is not. In a safe space, there is a designation that homophobic, biphobic, and transphobic language and actions are strictly forbidden. In a brave space, it goes beyond this. Experts have realized that while it is crucial to stop horrible things from being said, it is insufficient to stop there. In a safe space, a homophobic statement is responded to by telling the student that this is not acceptable, and ending that type of talk. In a brave-space setting, the conversation is much different. Instead of shutting the conversation down, those in brave spaces encourage further discussion about what has been said or done. Rather than saying that it is not acceptable to use a word or phrase, it is asked why the person chose to use that word or phrase. The focus is not on shutting down the communication; it is on nurturing the communication so as to better understand the perspective of that person, and to encourage them to think through where their thoughts and ideas originate. Whether these are biased or bigoted, and no matter how overarching these ideas and ideals are, starting the conversation where that person is at allows the speaker an opportunity to recognize the impact of their words, to consider where their assumptions began, and to make sure that what they have said is what they genuinely feel and intend when they are using this type of language.

In a school setting this may be somewhat tricky, because it is not always possible for an educator to stop an entire class to talk through this process with one student. It makes sense then that a safe-space protocol is used, as it is much more efficient to tell a student to be quiet than it would be to sit with them and talk through why they said what they did. However, these types of conversations can occur during a recess, in a study period before or after school, or you can assign them to write a paper that clarifies their words or requires them to research their incorrect assumptions about the person or group of people they spoke poorly about. In some classrooms, it may be best to establish a planned protocol at the beginning of the school term when all rules and expectations are being provided to and with the students. In elementary classes, it may be most appropriate to have the student draw or write about a time when their own feelings were hurt to help them recognize that what they say and do can help or hurt others. As students get older and become better writers, essays can be required that consider why the person said what they did, where the language came from, and the impact it may have on those who heard what was said. If a specific number of requirements, word count, or page length are provided in an age- and grade-appropriate manner, this can make it very quick for an educator to mandate this assignment without pausing classroom learning during class time.

When we look at the idea of safety, we must consider who is being kept safe. Politically, this can be a topic of significant debate. Often, this debate boils down to the difference between those who believe that people should not be forced to hear, see, or experience bigotry, and those who believe that shielding students from this experience makes them ill-prepared to deal with the real world and the things that people may say in public spaces or during their careers. It can be easy for a conversation about safety to become a conversation and debate over one side or the other. However, this is not necessary, nor is it helpful to students or educators.

This can lead to discussions about what safety measures are realistic. While some may feel that there should be significant opportunities for LGBT+ students or students of other minority groups to lead these conversations, this is not often possible. It is necessary as an educator to recognize that those in a position to make decisions about budgets may not be able to allocate programming or funds to one specific minority group within the school. However, it cannot be that nothing is done because action is said to be unaffordable. Instead, it is necessary to consider what changes and improvements can be made with little to no cost and with little to no change in the daily interactions of students and staff. These recommendations are much more likely to be approved by those in positions of power because they cause very little, if any, upset to predetermined budgets or to how educators and students typically behave.

Instead, educators can refer to existing school rules and policies. If there is already something in place regarding bullying, verbal assault, or physical assault, creating inclusion for LGBT+ people by making small changes becomes very simple. In some schools, support for LGBT+ people would be listed as a separate item within the school rules and guidelines. In other schools, they simply add the language "sexual orientation and gender identity" to rules that already list the types of bigotry or harassment that may exist, and which are not permitted. In today's society, most schools already have policies in place regarding sexually explicit words and actions, as well as gender biases, so including "sexual orientation and gender identity" or replacing previous words with these can make this policy much more inclusive, with very little change. This can result in a reasonably quick alteration without significant discussion or concern by the community or the school board.

In addition to this set of rules being a requirement of students to understand and follow, schools typically mandate educators be mindful of the rules and be held accountable for following them. Usually, this is because schools believe that educators are automatic role models and that following these rules is simply modeling appropriate adult behavior and interaction, which betters the school experience for everyone. It may be necessary to alert all staff in the district when a policy change is made or when additional words are added to existing policies. This allows everyone to recognize the change, and this will also enable educators and staff to be held accountable if they break these rules. These not only protect all LGBT+ students, but they also protect LGBT+ staff members, LGBT+ parents, and LGBT+ members of the community who may interact with the school through volunteer work, attending school assemblies or plays, and/or those who advertise with the school in academic award programs, athletic sponsorship, or when donating for school events. This protection keeps everyone physically and psychologically safe from discrimination and bigotry in school settings and at school events.

2

How to Be an LGBT+ Ally

Several educators may question whether there is a need for reading this book. These are typically either those who have personal feelings and beliefs about the LGBT+ community or those who already identify themselves as LGBT+ supporters. Those who have personal opinions and beliefs must recognize that it is against codes of conduct and professional codes of ethics to do less for one group of students than another or to allow one's personal beliefs or opinions to negatively influence the educational experience that students receive. It is also likely in the contract signed to become an educator that there is something in the policy that prevents educators from adversely interacting with students, staff, parents, and community members based on their minority status(es). This means that even if a reader of this book has powerful beliefs against the LGBT+ community or against students who self-identify as LGBT+, it is not permissible to avoid this topic. Instead, the information within this book can help both those with negative beliefs with opposition and those who already identify as LGBT+ supporters to best understand how to use their platform as educators to provide the best possible environment and experience for all, including the LGBT+ community.

The idea of identifying as an ally of any marginalized group of people is not new. While many may consider themselves to be an "LGBT+ ally," there is significant difference across the spectrum of ally identities. For others, this book may require more introspection to identify how and why their personal beliefs, opinions, and actions may influence their treatment of LGBT+ students, school staff, and school community leaders. Regardless of what identity a reader of this book wears, being mindful of that identity is not enough. Instead, we must examine what it means to be someone who supports the LGBT+ community, whether this is due to a personal conviction or mandates by the profession, the school district, and/or policies and laws.

This leads to questioning who qualifies as an ally. What makes a person qualified to identify as someone supportive of this community? This is something that may be debatable. In some cases, a person may identify themselves as an ally by simply not going out of their way to harm an LGBT+ person. Others may think that their ally status applies because they vote in each election in favor of inclusive policies. While neither of these is incorrect, and both benefit the LGBT+ community, this is not enough. Some debate whether the word "ally" is the best descriptor of a person regarding the LGBT+ community and their impact on it. While "ally" is the most commonly used word, some use the word "advocate," which implies much more of an active experience. To be an ally simply means to not go against this group of people. To be an advocate would acknowledge speaking up with or for LGBT+ people in situations where there may not be an LGBT+ person present, or where it may not be safe for an LGBT+ person to be out. Those who do more may be considered an "activist." Typically, this is a person who participates in different layers and levels of supporting the LGBT+ community. This may mean that the person talks with school boards or local, state, or federal politicians regarding better protections for LGBT+ people. In organizations that actively work to prevent equality for LGBT+ people, allies, advocates, and activists may be referred to as "accomplices." In the same way that a person who commits a crime may have an accomplice who helps them to commit a crime, the word "accomplice" is used to draw negative connotations to anyone who works to support the LGBT+ community.

How do you let people know that you are supportive? This is something that is much more introspective. Although we've discussed when this support is mandated by your profession, by your professional association, and by the rules and regulations you agreed to in order to become an educator in your specific school, how you support and how you let people know that you support is much more personal.

This leads us to consider how much you will stand up in support of the LGBT+ community. Is there something you are willing to say, but if you get a certain amount of pushback, you will sit quietly? This can cause us to ask: What are you willing to risk? Is there a line for you regarding who you are willing to upset, or how much you are willing to speak up and where you could be silenced? This is not rooted in judgment; different people have different priorities.

In some cases, it might be less risky for a person who has additional income to speak more loudly in support of the LGBT+ community because they are not financially risking their ability to pay their bills. In other situations, a person may have to choose whether to risk being suspended or terminated at work to support the LGBT+ community. While this is not intended to create a hierarchy of support among you and your colleagues, this is an internal or even a family conversation you may wish to have in advance so that you can make these decisions during a time at home rather than in the middle of a debate or problem situation.

Another question to consider is whether you would be willing to accept the stigma that comes with an LGBT+ identity. Often, our society believes that people only fight for those who are like them. It can cause people to question the personal identity of allies, advocates, or activists working for any marginalized groups. However, it is often much easier to see a person not identifying with a group they support when this differentiation is visible and prominent. For example, a white person participating in a protest or discussion for Black Lives Matter does not at any time appear to be a person of color. Since identifying as LGBT+ is not always visually apparent, supporting this community may cause some to make assumptions about one's sexual orientation or gender identity. Thus, it is essential to consider how far you may be willing to go to support a community and at what point, if ever, you will feel the need to separate yourself from the community by making it clear to others that you are not a member of that community.

In some cases, this may feel like simply being honest or even showing others that this population deserves support and acceptance from everyone, not just from other LGBT+ people. In different situations, becoming vocal about one's own gender identity or sexual orientation becomes a way to lessen the risk or minimize any backlash of participation of support. Again, there may not be a correct answer, but this is something you may wish to think through or talk through before events occur in which decisions would need to be made on this topic.

Let's look at mistakes that are often made by those who do indeed mean well and are supportive of LGBT+ people. This is not intended to cause you to second-guess your support in the future, or to come down hard on yourself if you realize anything that follows may indicate a mistake you have made in the past. This is intended to shine a light on areas that may not have been highlighted and to provide new considerations for supportive behaviors moving forward.

Do you tell your colleagues if somebody identifies as LGBT+? Is this something that you tell because it is exciting gossip? Is this something that you discuss with the intention of preventing somebody from making a homophobic, biphobic, or transphobic comment in front of a person who identifies as LGBT+? While the aim here may be right, it is never appropriate to talk about a person's sexuality or their gender unless they have given you specific permission to do so. Although you may mean well, this can create situations in which safety may become an issue for an LGBT+ person because there are some who do become violent, and because it means that the LGBT+ person does not know exactly who is aware of their identity. In addition, many states of America still allow a person to be fired for identifying as LGBT+. Even in cases where you think you are being helpful and where you absolutely mean well, outing an LGBT+ person at any time can put them at significant risk. Outing them in a workplace or to anyone who also works there can result in them losing their job. While this may not seem like a realistic situation because you know your colleagues, it is not always clear whose personal beliefs may cause them to create problems for an LGBT+ person.

Do you support equality specifically for the accolades and praise? While many people like to complete volunteer work or attend events in support of a minority group, it is essential to consider whether you would continue to support these organizations, people, and events even if you were never thanked, noticed, or praised for your support. Do you speak up when you hear bigotry? With its ongoing and consistent reports of violence against those in the LGBT+ community, the news has made it clear how frequently hate crimes occur. This means that anyone speaking up to support LGBT+ people in a public setting is taking a risk. This may be a minimal risk, or it may be more serious—for example, when involved in witnessing a violent act or some type of harassment against LGBT+ people. Do you have a line at which you stop supporting and stop helping? Acknowledging this in advance can help to prepare you for situations where you may have something occurring in front of you.

Too often, people do not think through what they would do in a situation until they are in that situation. That can lead to feeling uncertain of how to respond or not responding at all. In these situations, someone's safety may be directly threatened.

Knowing in advance how you would respond can help the person being victimized either because you choose to step in or because you are quickly able to find an alternative solution to help that person. Another consideration is whether and how much you would speak up in support of LGBT+ students and colleagues when it comes to your own family. It is common for people to be willing to step up or speak up when something is occurring in a public space between strangers. This is often because right and wrong can appear obvious. Plus, many people are not very concerned with what a stranger may think if they speak up. However, what about your own loved ones? Do you speak up if your spouse or child says something against LGBT+ people in their workplace or school? Do you speak up at a holiday meal when someone in your extended family says something negative about LGBT+ people? Often, there are no clear-cut answers. However, this may be a conversation to have with those you are closest to in advance, or before a large family gathering. In some cases, it may not make sense to challenge a grandparent in the moment. However, you may make the decision to address it with that person and with others at a different time.

Being mindful of this before the event can help to prevent anyone from believing that your silence in the moment equals an agreement to what was just said. Finally, do you self-identify to make sure that bigoted people know that you are not an LGBT+ person? While it may be intentional to identify otherwise when participating in political conversations, attending pride parades, or otherwise choosing to show that non-LGBT+ people also support LGBT+ people, it is also worth examining if there are times when you may want to self-identify so that you are not mistaken for an LGBT+ person. This leads back to the self-conversation of where the line of activism and support is for you.

Now that you have considered the above areas for yourself, within your relationship, within your family, and within your professional capacity, it is also important to identify ways in which it is possible to do better and to do more. Although there may be more LGBT+ representation in the media than ever before, the number of LGBT+ hate crimes that occur each year continues to grow. But this is a statistic that can be reversed with increased education of diversity and inclusion, which can lead to acceptance and lower experiences of violence.

One way to improve is to listen to your LGBT+ students and your LGBT+ colleagues. Being willing to hear the stories of LGBT+ people without interrupting them or turning the conversation back to you and your experiences allows that person to share their story and to feel heard as it is happening. While typical discussions are often a bit of a volley between participants listening and then sharing, specifically sharing experiences related to an LGBT+ identity can be very scary, especially for your students, who may be trying to discern whether or not you are a safe person they can trust. If a person decides to share with you, understand that they are trusting you with something significant. This is not meant to be the same sort of conversation as if you were discussing favorite bands; it is instead a way that you are being asked to absorb and take in their experience.

Next, learn from those lessons being shared, knowing that your LGBT+ students and LGBT+ colleagues are telling you something important. While it is common for people in majority groups to place the blame of negative interactions on minority members, listening to these stories can result in better understanding of how and why people are victimized. As is the case in any attack or victimization, it is never the victim's fault. It is never appropriate to ask a person why they didn't behave differently; it is instead necessary to validate that you have heard what they've shared, that you acknowledge their trust in you with a vulnerable part of themselves, and that you do not turn it into an opportunity to blame the victim for what someone else did to them.

Next, talk about it with others without outing the student or colleague. When you are talking with others about the issues and stigma that LGBT+ people face, be sure to keep the stories that you tell of other people's lives vague enough so that you are not outing those who shared with you to new people. You can start with "I have a student who…" or "I heard about a teacher at another school who…" If the details of the story are something you find necessary to be heard by others, discuss this with the person who shared with you. Ask them if they would be open to sharing their story. Offer to go with them and sit by them if they agree to share their story. Or, if they are unwilling or unable, ask them if they would help you figure out what part of the story they would feel comfortable with you sharing. This allows them to remain in control of their own experiences, their personal stories, and their own truth. Once you have received the information and experience that an LGBT+ person has shared with you, think about how you can use this new knowledge to help bring about more inclusion and better resolutions to minimize safety concerns.

Finally, donate your time and your support to your LGBT+ students and colleagues. Find ways to use the resources that you have to support inclusive policies and supportive programming. This may be by advising for a club or group that supports diversity and inclusion, it may be in encouraging the group or activity you chaperone to learn about LGBT+ people or current laws, or it may be by integrating LGBT+ leaders into your group's learning experience. This allows LGBT+ people the benefit of having a majority person on their side without it leading to a concern that you may breach their privacy, create unsafe situations for them, or turn the situation into something that is about you.

3

Privilege

There has been a lot of discussion and debate about what privilege means, both as a term and how it impacts an individual's life. In reality, almost all of us have some modicum of privilege, whether overt or not. In fact, nearly all of us also have some situations in which we lack privilege. The point of acknowledging privilege is not to put down people who were or were not born a certain way or to blame people with privilege for having it. It is simply meant to lead to mindfulness. This allows a person to recognize the ways in which they benefit, which may not be something they regularly (or ever) consider.

What counts as privilege?

Anything that you get the benefit of that others do not counts as privilege. For example, if you can walk, talk, see, breathe, and eat on your own, there is privilege. If you live where there is not a war occurring, if you were taught to read, if you have access to sanitary supplies (including tampons/pads, toilet paper, soap, etc.) and clean water, there is privilege. If, in television and films, you see couples and love stories of people of your gender and the gender of people you are attracted to, there is privilege. If you identify as the gender that matches your genitalia, there is privilege. If you are young or classically attractive or financially stable or well fed or have air conditioning in your home or have a working vehicle or have access to medication when you are unwell or own books or watch television or have a smartphone or know how to drive or have a choice of clothing in your closet or sleep in a comfortable bed or consistently have electricity or bathe in warm water or have a consistent address, those are all privileges.

Why does privilege matter?

Too often, a conversation about privilege becomes an argument over who has more privilege than whom, which privilege is better to have than which other privilege, or what negative experiences counteract which privileges. This makes sense because it can be easy to assume that recognizing having privilege would be the same as claiming to have no problems or no right to complain about having problems. That's simply unrealistic and it can certainly inflame a conversation quite quickly. However, recognizing our privileges can help us to become more mindful of those who do not have what we have, as well as helping to articulate our needs to those who have what we do not.

For example, by recognizing that not everyone in your school has consistent food access, a school or its staff member may become more aware of areas where wasted cafeteria food could be donated to those in need who may otherwise miss meals at home. By recognizing that not every student identifies as heterosexual, pamphlets and other sex education materials can be reviewed to ensure that all sexualities are included so that all students gain access to information about how to protect themselves and their partners during sex. By recognizing that not all students may be open about their sexuality, a health class teacher, guidance counselor, or other caring staff member may find a place to put these pamphlets and resource materials that is private enough so that all students can access them without having to do so in front of peers. By recognizing that the school may have not yet experienced a lawsuit by an LGBT+ student, family, or staff member for discrimination means that the school can begin to examine areas in which improvement is needed, and there is an opportunity to make these changes before or without creating conflict or legal ramifications because of the poor experience of an LGBT+ person.

In short, the purpose of defining one's privilege as an individual, as a department, as a school, or as a school district is not to belittle or undermine occurring problems or stressors. It is simply to examine the ways in which the existing structure and schema benefit some while being detrimental to others. Once this awareness is obtained, it can be easy to begin to assess where there are areas that can be improved upon, which can lead to change, and which in turn can lead to a more inclusive and affirming school for all.

4

Intersectionality

Although the definition section is intended to be all-encompassing, it seems inappropriate not to provide a separate place to discuss and recognize intersectionality. Coined by Kimberlé Williams Crenshaw in 1989, the term identifies the intersection of being a member of more than one minority group. It recognizes that each group's membership comes with its own struggles and that the intersection of two or more memberships is more than simply the sum of society's mistreatment of each group within which a person identifies. The definition in this context is acknowledging that although an LGBT+ identity is, in itself, a minority status, many individuals exist within the intersection of two or more minority groups, which directly impacts their school experiences.

As one can imagine, each group that they are a part of causes them to be the target of misunderstanding and injustice, and to be at a higher risk of being victimized. The comic Wanda Sykes has built this into many of her comedy routines and interviews she has given, as she identifies as female, Black, and a lesbian. Her appearance allows the general public to assume her to be female and to identify her skin tone, leaving her already in a minority group at the intersection of female and Black. This individual exists at the intersection of female and Black and gay, creating three ways in which others may be biased against her, further causing her and others with this shared intersectionality to be that much more discriminated against than someone with only one of those three minority statuses, which is more discrimination than someone without any of these minority statuses faces.

In some cases, the identity of intersectionality may appear obvious. In other cases, there may be minority group status that may be more difficult for the casual observer to identify. In addition, there may be an assumption that certain members of certain minority groups may not identify as LGBT+. Typically, this occurs when one or more minority identifications lead the individual to be desexualized by society. One example of desexualized or infantilized groups is that of people with significant physical and/or learning disabilities. Through media portrayal and the additional need of assistance to perform daily tasks, it is common for society to see individuals with physical limitations as patients, as helpless, and/or as people to be pitied. This makes it difficult for many to recognize any gender identity or sexual orientation in association with that individual or an entire group of individuals with the same characteristics. This can result in a lack of representation for LGBT+ individuals who have obvious physical limitations. The deaf community is another group where members are often not considered to also be in a gender or sexual minority. While our society has been making strides to recognize that hard-of-hearing or deaf people live rich, full lives, it remains prevalent in the media that individuals of this minority group are seen as being in need of assistance or being victims of crimes.

Although this book focuses on making schools more LGBT+ inclusive, this is not intended to be done at the detriment of recognition of other minority groups or their needs. Focusing on this particular group and its needs can also provide you with insights and tools to become more mindful of the needs of students and staff who are part of other minority groups. Use what you gain via this book to encourage you to think about how different students may need similar types of support and how you can be a more inclusive colleague.

Battle fatigue

As you move through this book, giving yourself time to pause periodically and reflect, you are encouraged to consider not just how the information impacts your life and your actions but also how the lack of knowledge and the need to educate others has impacted LGBT+ students, families, and staff. Too often, a person in a minority group is expected to provide insights to others. There can be an expectation that it is incumbent upon a person in a persecuted group to raise their hand, explain their identity, explain how the current statement or situation is inappropriate, offer suggestions, recommend a solution, and implement the new course of action.

It is also necessary to consider that laws and law enforcement may already be against them. (This is not to discount areas where non-discrimination policies exist or the many wonderful police officers; this is simply to acknowledge how many areas of the nation lack even basic LGBT+ protections and how many stories exist where officers have been unkind or downright cruel to LGBT+ people.) There is also a significant amount of bigotry that exists, especially for those whose identities are at the intersection of a number of minority groups. This means that there may never be a time when the individual is able to truly relax because they are forced to always be in fear for their safety and their lives, spending a significant portion of their energy simply trying to stay alive, before they can even begin to add other areas of focus to their day.

As such, it is easy for a person to become exhausted from trying to meet or manage the expectations others have of them, while being seen as the voice of their entire minority group and while trying to avoid becoming the victim of violence. For students, they are often juggling this while also attempting to figure out their own identity and place in the world and meet the requirements placed upon them during the learning process. For families, they are often juggling all of the multitudes of parental requirements alongside judgment from others and stress of safety risks. For LGBT+ employees, their jobs become that much more difficult when they are not only at risk as people but even more so in areas where it is legal for them to be fired for their identity, which means that they consistently also live in fear of sudden job and income loss.

Siblings and families of LGBT+ people may also experience this fatigue. Families may be forced to forever defend their child's identity to adults to ensure appropriate educational opportunities and treatment in schools. Siblings may spend much of their time in school defending their LGBT+ sibling, monitoring whether their sibling is safe from bullying, or fending off those who mistreat them because they have an LGBT+ sibling. This can result in significant and ongoing efforts by everyone to keep the LGBT+ person as safe and respected as possible.

As you move through this book and as you become more mindful of the experiences of LGBT+ people, you are encouraged to take time to think about when you personally have felt most unsafe, in danger, or at risk of violence. You are asked to think about how it felt when you were called down to the boss's office. You are asked to think about how your life would change if you were to be suddenly fired at this very moment. How would each of these situations feel?

As you consider each of these and the impact they would have on your life, you are encouraged to imagine the experience of living full-time in that feeling. You are asked to then consider how much additional strength it would take to feel this way and then complete your daily tasks and meet the expectations given to you by others. Finally, consider how it might feel if there was a person you could spend time with and a place you could go where those fears were lifted, where your safety was affirmed, and where your goals were supported. This is where you can begin to understand just how much of an impact you, your classroom, your school, and your school district can have on LGBT+ youth, LGBT+ families, and LGBT+ staff.

5

Terminology

As we get ready to begin, people may be on very different levels of understanding about the topics of this book. Additionally, some people believe they understand more than they do, and others probably understand more than they think they do. In a desire for everyone to begin on the same page, let's start off talking about terminology so that we all move forward together through the rest of the book.

Before we begin with current knowledge, let's take a moment to discuss the history of the naming of this group of people. We used to see the abbreviation that GLBT (gay, lesbian, bisexual, transgender); now we typically see it as LGBT+ (lesbian, gay, bisexual, transgender). Why? Many women's groups argue that GLBT is yet another place where men are placed before women, so it is often considered more inclusive to place "lesbian" before "gay" as in "LGBT." However, as society and science begin to indicate that gender and sexuality may be more of a spectrum than a set number of boxes a person may check, it is becoming more common to see it listed as LGBT+. That allows for keeping the acronym short while also being the most inclusive possible.

What do professional sources say? This is really crucial because it considers the awareness that the LGBT+ population exists and why it exists, based on fact and on medical research. Too often, when talking about this population, there is an expectation that people's opinions should dictate how others are perceived. Instead, however, it is vital that we consider what professional associations say about this area in order to ensure that we are behaving based on best practices from science and research, rather than our own personal opinions, biases, or beliefs. (This is not to say that we can't acknowledge that we have our own opinions, biases, and beliefs; it is simply to indicate that although we have those, it is not our place as educators to impose them on others.)

When looking at this from an educator perspective, we have to consider the ways in which our own personal behavior toward and treatment of those who identify as LGBT+ may be hindering their ability to learn and fully contribute to the academic community of our school, school district, and overall community.

Let's look at appropriate terminology. This is something that does change often, so you may see some terms that used to not be accepted now being used, and you may also see that some terms that used to be accepted no longer are. Let's start with the umbrella terms first and then work into what falls under those umbrellas.

Sexual orientation: This refers to someone's sexual and romantic attraction. Most people have a sexual orientation. (Someone who does not is called asexual.) You can be attracted (romantically, emotionally, and/or sexually) to people of the opposite gender and identify as "straight" or "heterosexual," or be attracted to people of the same gender and identify as "gay" or "lesbian." You can also be attracted to people of either gender, which is called "bisexual." Some people identify as being attracted to a person regardless of their gender. This person would identify as "pansexual." Some people question whether a sexual experience is required for a person to know their orientation. Although each individual is unique, there are plenty of middle school and high school students who identify their sexual orientation based on the feelings that they have, even if they have not had actual physical contact of a sexual nature.

Gender identity: Gender identity refers to a person's internal sense of being male, female, somewhere in between, or somewhere completely outside of the gender binary. For many people, one's gender identity corresponds with their biological facts; in other words, a person has female genitalia, and female DNA, and they identify as female. That makes the person cisgender. On the other hand, a person who identifies as transgender is someone who has external genitalia and DNA that do not match how that person sees themselves and how they identify in the world.

Gender expression: Gender expression relates to how a person chooses to communicate their gender identity to others through their clothing, hairstyles, manners, and behaviors. This may be conscious or subconscious. While most people's understanding of gender expression relates to masculinity and femininity, the expressions of these can occur in a myriad of ways, typically related to the impact of product marketing, mass media, and gender norms that date back generations. This is why we identify things like lace and glitter as being feminine and things like leather as being more masculine. Some people may choose an item specifically to broadcast their gender identity, and others may choose it because they enjoy it or like the way it feels, even if it does not necessarily correlate with their gender identity.

To summarize, sexual orientation describes who you feel sexually/romantically/emotionally attracted to. Gender identity is the gender that you feel in your brain regardless of your genitalia. Gender expression is what clothing, hairstyle, and mannerisms your conscious or subconscious mind chooses when you present yourself to the world.

Now that we've covered the overarching umbrella terminology, let's look at the terminology under these umbrellas.

Gay: A man who is romantically and sexually attracted to other males. This may also be used as a term that is more inclusive which would encompass gay men, lesbians, and people who identify as bisexual.

Lesbian: A woman whose romantic and sexual attraction is to other women.

Bisexual: A person who is sexually/romantically/emotionally attracted to both men and women, though not necessarily simultaneously. A bisexual person may not be attracted equally to both genders, and the degree of attraction may change over time.

Let's talk about gender! In present-day American society, there is an overarching norm that gender is binary—that is, that there are two options (male or female). This is decided based on external genitalia.

This is what is announced at "gender reveal parties," as it is based on whether the fetus does or does not have a penis. Sex and gender are not the same thing. Sex is the chromosomal designation of a person's genetics, whereas gender is a social construct. In other words, it *should* be called a "sex reveal party," since no one will know how the child identifies their gender for some time yet!

How is gender guided by society? This begins before a person is even born. It includes when people ask whether the baby is a boy or a girl. It includes when parents begin to envision their child's future extra-curricular activities (football or ballet, fixing cars or going shopping). It is often used to decide themes for baby showers, to send baby gifts, and to decorate nurseries. Pink and lace for girls; blue and trucks for boys. Check out the baby and child aisles in stores and you'll see this on full display: lace and ruffles for girls, reinforced knees on pants for boys. Hair and makeup toys in pink packages for girls; wrestling action figures and superheroes in blue packages for boys. In the tween and teen sections of stores, girls' areas are often filled with sparkly jewelry, whereas boys' sections have items meant not to stain easily. Everywhere you look, society shows that girls must be petite, delicate, and appearance-based, and boys are meant to be rough and tumble. While this may not be news to you, have you ever considered that society is also showing that there are only two genders?

What is gender? Gender is the way a person identifies their place in a spectrum of masculine and feminine, or outside of that spectrum altogether. How do people identify themselves within this spectrum?

Transgender: A broad term meaning that a person's gender identity does not match their assigned gender at birth.

Cisgender: A term to describe a person whose gender identity does match their assigned gender at birth. This means that transgender and cisgender are opposite terms.

Gender non-binary: A term to describe a person who identifies as a gender that is not male or female but may be a combination of the two or something different. (You may hear this abbreviated as "NB" and/or see this abbreviated in writing as "enby"—the phonetic pronunciation of NB. As the abbreviation of "NB" has long been in use in communities of color to indicate "non-Black," "enby" is the most inclusive written form of abbreviation for non-binary.)

Gender fluid: A term to describe a person whose gender identity may change or evolve over time. This goes beyond a desire to wear a dress one day and pants the next, as this is not about gender expression and clothing or hairstyle but rather about the identity of a person and how they are in their gender from day to day.

Agender: A term to describe a person who does not identify as having a gender.

These identities are also why we have added the + to the LGBT+ in our language, and why you will typically see more recent publications or speeches referring to this population as LGBT+.

Note: Transgender, cisgender, gender non-binary, gender fluid, and agender are adjectives, not nouns. Just like Black, Asian, Hispanic, short, and tall. There is no such word as "transgender*ed*," as the word is not a verb, so it cannot have a past tense. Always put the word "person" after the gender-identifying word, as this is a word to describe someone. This is just the way you don't see a "short," you see a "short person." You may see the term "male to female transgender person" or "female to male transgender person." This has been used for quite some time to first identify the person's gender assigned at birth and second identify the gender the person identifies as. For example, a "male to female transgender person" would indicate that the person was assumed by others to be a male person at birth (due to external genitalia) and now identifies and/or lives as a female person.

However, updated terminology has also caused some to redefine the categorization of transgender people because science is indicating that gender is being seen more and more as a social construct. This would mean that nobody is born with a gender, since nobody is born with an innate sense of social construct. With that in mind, the terminology is being changed. Now, the identity of a transgender person is typically described as "assigned female at birth" (AFAB) or "assigned male at birth" (AMAB).

Questions and answers

Q: How do I know what to call someone if I think they might be LGBT+?

A: If you aren't sure what name to call someone, ask for their name, and they'll tell you. This is the same for any person whose name you forgot. This is also the same for someone who was named Carter Joel, who prefers to be called CJ. This isn't something specific to the LGBT+ community, although many feel anxious out of fear of offending a person in the LGBT+ community. In this case, when it comes to someone's name, it is just the same as anyone else's name, but you do not know, do not remember, or cannot recall what version of their name they may choose to go by.

Q: What about pronouns? How do I know whether to use he or she or...?

A: If you are uncertain about pronouns, ask, "What pronouns do you use?" It is considered most appropriate to ask the question that way, rather than to ask, "What is your preferred pronoun?" This is because "preferred" indicates that this is about preference and not about identity. You're not asking a person which version of a pronoun they might prefer, like the way you may ask me if I prefer chocolate or vanilla ice cream and I might like one more than the other. Instead, you are asking what pronoun they use, just the way that someone might ask what racial background you are or height you are; this is not what a person prefers—it is who they are. You may hear someone introduce themselves with their name, followed by the pronouns they use. For example, when a person introduces themselves and includes their pronouns, they may say, "Hi, I'm Rachel, she, her, hers." That means that their name is Rachel and they identify using female pronouns. If you were to tell someone that this person agreed to go to the store, you would say, "*Rachel* said *she* can go to the store." If you said, "*Rachel* said *he* can go to the store," that would not feel right to them, and it would not be a fit with how they identify.

Some prefer to use a pronoun that is neither male nor female. The introduction to such a person would sound like, "Hi, I'm Melvin, they, them, theirs." On many computer programs, this will be underlined as a mistake because "they" and "theirs" are known to have been plural, and you are using the pronoun for one individual person. This may require you to correct your word processing program. This is because the English language has not yet offered a singular non-binary gender pronoun, although this is common in many other languages. However, the Merriam-Webster dictionary now accepts they/them/their as singular pronouns too.

Homophobia: The intense fear and hatred of or discomfort with people who love and are attracted to members of the same gender.

Transphobia: The intense fear and hatred of or discomfort with people whose gender identity or gender expression does not match or conform to cultural gender norms.

Internalized homophobia or transphobia: When self-identification of societal stereotypes results in a person hating who they are, causing them to dislike or resent their sexual orientation or gender identity.

Medical options for transgender people: This is a conversation that is necessary because educators may see the results of some of these different actions and choices in the transgender population within their school, whether with a student, staff member, or parent in the school's community.

Some mistakenly believe that medical options are easily acquired and happen quickly. In America, to be able to receive any medical intervention, the person must be consistently seen by a licensed mental health professional for many months or years, working in concert with a medical professional or team before any medical interventions can occur. In addition, health insurances do not typically cover any of these interventions, so many families spend years saving money to afford what is best for the individual. This means that although something may seem sudden to you, by the time you are aware of the change the family and individual have likely spent years being guided by multiple healthcare professionals. No one takes this lightly, and no medical interventions are offered or are an option until/unless multiple specifically trained gender professionals have done their work to ensure that this is the appropriate treatment for the person.

Not all transitions look the same.

For younger children, for example, long before puberty begins, transition may look like a child having a different haircut, wearing affirming clothing, and the teacher being asked to call the student by a different name. For example, this may mean that in kindergarten there was a little boy named Jason, who had short hair and wore blue clothing. That same child may attend the first grade with longer hair, wearing dresses, and the parents may ask the child to ask the teacher to call the child Alice. This is because very young children typically do not show gender characteristics other than the length of their hair, the style of their clothing, and their name. When this occurs, speak with your supervisor and make sure that there is a plan in place and a protocol for how to deal with children who identify as a gender they previously did not. By being mindful of this, and already having protocols in place, a lot of the confusion for the staff can be eliminated.

(This will come up again when having conversations later in this book about restrooms and other ways in which educators should be mindful so that transitioning children are not discriminated against intentionally or accidentally.)

At the middle-school level, the parents of a transgender child may be in the process of deciding if or when to begin puberty blockers. This is a type of medication that prevents the body from beginning adult puberty. This means that children assigned male at birth will not grow facial and body hair, their voice will not deepen, and their genitals will not grow. For a child assigned male at birth who identifies as female, this is vital. If not given puberty blockers, a person identifying as a girl would have to watch her body become increasingly more male in appearance. This can create extreme anxiety and depression. It may even result in suicide attempts. For children assigned female at birth, puberty blockers prevent the body shape from changing at a time when hips would become wider and breasts would begin to grow. This can make a person who identifies as male become incredibly uncomfortable and feel unsafe in a body that is growing increasingly dissimilar to their gender identity. It can be a very unsafe time for a transgender child if puberty blockers are not provided.

When high school begins, it is common that, in addition to blocking the puberty hormones that are not congruent with gender identity, hormones will begin to be introduced that encourage the body to develop in a way that aligns with the person's identity. This means beginning testosterone for people assigned female at birth who identify as male. That testosterone will do what it does in cisgender male teenagers: it will cause the voice to deepen, facial and body hair to begin to grow, and all other male physical characteristics to begin to develop. For children assigned male at birth, the hormone introduced is estrogen, which allows for a more feminine shape, the raising of the voice pitch, and for breasts to begin to grow. In situations in which children identify as transgender before puberty and have affirming and supportive parents, the use of puberty blockers followed by gender-confirming hormones can result in a child that appears to the public to be the gender in which they identify, though their genitalia may not match. In situations in which the family is not affirming, these children may become increasingly unsafe and this can increase the risk of self-harm or suicidality. Some may attempt to remove genitalia, and others may seek out illegal hormone blockers or hormone replacements in hopes of preventing their body from changing due to their natural hormones. In situations in which parents are not affirming, while hormone blockers and new hormones cannot simply be provided by the school, it will be necessary that educators be very mindful of the mental health of these children and work with them to make plans in order to ensure their safety.

(Later, this book will guide you toward setting up a safer school system, as these students may struggle with being bullied by peers who are aware that they are transgender, even if the student presents as the gender in which they identify.)

Although it is common that people are interested in this type of hormonal impact on someone, it is never ever okay to ask a person to disclose what hormones, if any, they may be taking. The only reason for this to be asked/known is if the school nurse is inquiring specifically to meet an individual's medical needs at school, or if the student chooses to volunteer this information. While it is normal and typical for educators to be interested, especially those who lack insight into this process, it is not the student's role to educate their teachers. Instead, refer to this book and its resources to find out more without creating a situation in which the student feels obligated to disclose or unsafe. In addition, surgeries are probably not happening at the K–12 level for students. This is because their bodies are still changing and growing, and most surgeons are not likely to perform a surgical procedure of any sort on anyone under the age of 17. However, it is possible or even likely that among school staff, faculty, student's parents, and other community leaders, there will be those who identify as transgender. They may have or may not have had any type of hormonal intervention or surgeries. This may include genital reconstruction surgery (typically referred to as gender confirmation surgery, though this terminology does change frequently); breast implants; the shaving down of an Adam's apple; a brow lift and shaving of the brow bone, or another surgery to feminize the face of a person assigned male at birth; or fat injections, breast reduction or chest reconstruction, and other options for people to appear more masculine for those assigned female at birth. Some identify a part of their body as not being congruent with their identity and thus want to make changes as quickly as medically possible. Others simply do not connect those aspects of their body to being related to gender the way that many do. At no time is it ever appropriate to ask about which surgeries, if any, a person has had. The only people who need to know that information are the person and their medical practitioners.

A transgender person is not "more trans" or "less trans" based on how far through a transition process the person is. Some people choose never to take hormones and never to have surgery, others only choose to utilize some of the treatment options, and others choose to alter their physical appearance without utilizing any hormonal or surgical options. This is a personal choice based on their own feelings about their bodies and based on financial options available.

Some people believe that they can identify a transgender person simply by looking at them. While this might have been largely true in past generations because there was no opportunity to utilize hormones and surgical options, the idea that this is an obvious identity is incredibly outdated, and the imagery that people use is incredibly biased. There are many people who identify as transgender, gender non-conforming, or gender non-binary whose appearance may give no indication of their gender identity. It is not their obligation to provide this information to you. You may have access to this information if the school has the child listed under one name and gender but the child presents and identifies differently. In these cases, make sure to communicate with your supervisor in order to make sure that the name and pronouns within the classroom for the student are what they have asked to be called. You may also wish to speak with your supervisor about changing the name and pronoun on the attendance sheets in order to ensure that substitute teachers or other guests in the classroom do not misgender the student. Remember that a transgender person is just like any other person; their bodies and their choices with their bodies are none of your business unless you are a medical professional and the question you are asking is medically necessary. While you may have questions, it is not the individual's job to teach you, nor is it appropriate for you to expect such. If, however, you are unsure, ask the student privately and follow their lead. Never ask a person of any age about this information or anything related to their identity in front of others. It is already very difficult for transgender people of all ages to avoid bullying or violence, and putting the spotlight on their identity in front of others may make the situation much harder for them.

Some associate the idea of a transgender person with being a drag queen. They're very, very different. Drag queens and drag kings are biological males and females respectively who present as members of the other sex specifically to perform or entertain. The performance may include singing, lip-synching, or dancing. Drag performers may or may not identify as transgender. Many drag queens and kings identify as gay, lesbian, or bisexual. This is very different from a transgender person, whose heart and mind are of a gender that is different than their genitalia and who is living as themselves. Transgender people do not do this for the entertainment or amusement of others; it is simply who the person is. As an example, this is the difference between the way you may choose to dress up for Halloween and your identity every day; one is meant to be fun and entertaining, and the other simply is who you are.

While it used to be very rare for anybody to openly identify as LGBT+, the past decade has significantly changed this. Members of boy bands including members of New Kids on the Block and

*NSYNC have come out as gay. Sonny and Cher's son has come out as a transgender man, living openly, and with the support of his parents. Top musicians have also identified themselves as bisexual, or lesbian, taking their partners with them to very public events. This can be incredibly helpful and affirming for those in the LGBT+ community; however, the social change of people feeling more able to be out and live openly does not mean that bullying does not happen. In order to prevent bullying in the school and in general, allies are necessary.

Helpful hints

It is important to hear and understand terminology from the perspective of those you are engaging in conversation with. For young people, the terminology presented here often provokes romantic notions and ideas of identity and self-discovery, rather than the political or sexual context these words may evoke for older audiences. Using a person's chosen term without judgment can make all the difference in the world. This means being open at all times, regardless of whether you understand why a child in your classroom has chosen to identify by a different name, gender, or a pronoun from those they have previously used in your classroom or in your school. The best course of action is to thank them for letting you know and then to use that name and pronoun when calling on them in class. If other students question this, not every moment needs to be a reason to stop the class for a long lecture about these topics. It may simply be that you can say that this is the name this student is using and then continue with your class. If you accept this information from the student and behave as if it is no big deal, it is much more likely that the other students in the class will behave as if it is no big deal as well. However, be mindful of what may be being whispered when you are at the front of the class or things that might be said in the hallway before or after class. You can always check in with a student before or after class to ask if they are feeling safe and supported or to remind them that your classroom is a place where they will not be judged or mistreated.

Lesbians

It should not be assumed that lesbians have never been sexually active with men; we cannot assume when talking with students at middle school or high school that they have not had sexual encounters with males. Making this assumption can leave them unsafe due to lack of information given, because there is an assumption that information is not useful. The risks of suicidal ideation, self-harm, and depression may be higher in lesbians and bisexual individuals, especially those who are not open about their sexual orientation, who are not in satisfying and safe relationships, and/or who lack social support. Smoking and obesity rates are also higher in lesbians and bisexual women because smoking and eating are inexpensive ways in which some cope, and this population may be more likely to need coping mechanisms to deal with the stress of living in a world that is often homophobic and biphobic.

In addition, many lesbian and bisexual women are victims of hate crimes, and they often fear for their safety. Intimate partner violence may also occur between women in same-sex relationships at a rate that is similar to heterosexual relationships. Lesbian women can also be raped, physically assaulted, or stalked by a female partner. It may be difficult for students to be open about this, especially if they do not feel supported at home and within the school. They may struggle with addressing these concerns and their relationships out of fear that they will not be believed, or that people will assume that women cannot be as violent toward each other as men have been known to be violent in interactions with women. If a student comes to you with concerns about relationship safety, it is necessary that you follow the same protocol the school has for opposite-sex relationships and for any report of violence whatsoever.

Gay and MSM

This categorizes male-identified people who have sexual encounters and/or relationship with other male-identified people. At the present time, some see "gay" as an identity that deals with a specific type of personality or type of behaviors. In those cases, some do not identify as "gay" but rather as "MSM"—men who have sex with men. (This may be how a male-identified student identifies his sexuality, even if his age and/or appearance do not yet make him a "man" by definition.) Regardless of a person's chosen label, there is still an increased risk for this population of sexually transmitted infections (STIs) as well as psychological and behavioral disorders related to their experiences and whether or not they are accepted at home. It may be easy to find statistics that indicate that gay men or men who have sex with men are contracting more STIs than other groups; however, this research is often heavily biased either in the way the study was written to bolster pre-existing misperceptions or by misinterpreting the results to further a person or group's agenda, regardless of the breadth of research that indicates otherwise.

This may be because the people funding the study have personal or religious feelings about homosexuality. It may be because a drug company is biased in their studies in an attempt to indicate a need for a drug they are trying to sell. It may also be that the place in which these studies occur is heavily biased toward or against one type or group of people. For example, doing a study while inside a nightclub will likely only capture the responses of people who go to nightclubs; it will not also include people who do not go to nightclubs, which may be a significantly different experience. This detail is important to know, so that you can both consider your own biases and beliefs and have an understanding that parents of students may make assumptions based on biased research that can cause them to be not accepting and not affirming of their children. With this in mind, homosexuality has been associated with a higher risk of psychological and behavioral disorders, including depression, anxiety disorders, suicidal thoughts and plans, eating disorders, alcohol and substance abuse, and cigarette smoking. The stigmatization of homosexuality in American society results in the frequent exposure of homosexual men to discrimination and victimization. This is believed to be a causative factor in the development of psychological and behavioral disorders.

In bisexual people, it is a common misconception that a person who identifies as bisexual is either "greedy" or uncertain. Others believe that a person identified as bisexual is actually gay, but they are not yet ready to admit that. This is inaccurate. There has been no single pattern to prove this assumption. Some bisexual-identified people feel they fit into neither the heterosexual nor homosexual world, while others feel identified more predominantly as being attracted to one gender identity than the other. Due to a lack of understanding, acceptance, or even knowledge of the bisexual identity, the failing relationship issues facing bisexual people seldom emerge when contemplating policy and legal changes. Some bisexual people have legally married opposite-sex partners. As a result, they are able to access the privileges afforded to married couples. However, many bisexual people are not married. They may choose not to get married, or their family may not be accepting of their union. Some may wish to become parents regardless of their marital status. Bisexual people often face similar discrimination and obstacles to those faced by gay and lesbian people in regard to custody, visitation, or adoption of children. This means that in addition to your students possibly identifying as bisexual, you may have students who are dealing with parents who identify as lesbian, gay, bisexual, or transgender.

Not only is this something students are learning about as they become more clear in their own sexuality, but this may also be impacting the custody agreements about them if the parents have already been divorced, or it may lead to parents being divorced. It is necessary to be respectful of this and to be mindful that this may be an aspect of the student's personal life which may impact their behaviors and their abilities in the classroom, not because they do not care or because they are too lazy to complete their homework, but because they may have these trials going on at home which may be too much of a distraction and emotional burden to manage while being able to complete all assignments on time.

Transgender

People generally experience gender identity and sexual orientation as two different things. Sexual orientation refers to one's sexual attraction to others, whereas gender identifies a reference to one's sense of oneself in their own identity. Usually, the gender that the individual is attracted to does not change when a person begins to live openly as a transgender person. For example, a person assigned male at birth who is attracted to women will be attracted to women after transitioning, when they openly identify as female. This will mean that this person who was once seen by society as a heterosexual man would now be seen by the world as a lesbian.

When looking at estimates for how many LGBT+ people there are in any given city, state, or country, it is very difficult to accurately account for this. This is because there is often bias in the accounting experience, and it also requires a person not only to be out but also to trust the survey taker with this personal information. This can lead to statistics that are much lower than are actually accurate in terms of how many people identify as LGBT+ in America today.

When working with a transgender student, a few tips

Number one, it isn't always about the student's transgender status. It is important not to focus so narrowly on the fact that a person is transgender that you end up making that characteristic more important than the actual reason the student is seeking your help. It is important that you help your student focus on the real issue and steer them away from focusing on their gender identity if that is not the core problem. For example, if a transgender student is struggling with their math homework, it is important to focus on the math homework and the struggle related to math. It would make sense in some cases to be mindful that the child may have some additional struggles simultaneously due to their gender identity. However, it is also very likely that this is a student simply struggling in a math class, just the way so many cisgender students do. By focusing on math concerns, it allows the student to be guided appropriately without ignoring the real issue of math difficulty, and without letting the student off the hook for incorrect math problems due to their transgender identity.

Second, be aware of the assumptions you are making about a person's gender. It is very common to assume that you know a person's gender or gender identity based on stereotypes. Some people's expression or identity is not stereotypical and may be different from what you would expect or assume. Therefore, it is important to be open to allow a person to self-identify. If you are unsure, it is appropriate to ask the person how they would like to be addressed. Often, this can be taken care of easily on the first day of school. Just as when you call roll you offer students the opportunity to identify the name they prefer to be called, the same can be true for transgender students. Just as a student named Elizabeth would tell you on the first day of school that she prefers to be called Liz or Lizzie or Beth, it is equally appropriate for a student named David to tell you that he prefers to be called Denise. Just as you would write that Elizabeth has asked to be called Liz, you should do the same for a transgender student so that all students in your classroom are spoken to and called on by the name that they go by. This allows for inclusive classrooms without doing anything that singles out a transgender student.

It is also important to be mindful of orientation assumptions. While most students do identify as heterosexual, not all do. This means that if a student is talking about someone they are dating, do not assume that the student is speaking of someone of a different gender. Making these assumptions or making jokes in class may seem light and fun but they could put a target on a student who needs to lie about their life for the class to move on, or may cause them to feel as if they are in a classroom where it may not be safe. Instead, you can simply remind all students that talking about their date on Friday night is not a conversation meant to be happening in the middle of your history class and encourage them to focus and get back to work, just as you would any other student talking about any other date.

It is also important to know the laws. This is a constantly changing situation. While this is not always something that everyone can keep up with, it may make sense in your school for the supervisor or principal to assign one person whose job it is to be mindful of changes. This can create a protocol in which legal changes can be sent by email to the entire staff so that everyone is aware. In addition, if you live in a state in which the laws are less than inclusive and respectful, this does not require you *not* to be inclusive or respectful. You can always curate the school system, a school building, and/or your classroom to be a place in which a student can be authentically themselves.

Next, except in rare cases, it is very important that you use the name and the pronoun that corresponds to that person's gender identity. In addition, your student may choose to use a name that is gender-neutral or associated with the opposite gender for the pronoun; it is important to be aware of and respect this. This may mean that someone named Brian prefers to be called Brian, but uses female pronouns. This may mean that your student prefers to be called Sam—a name that does not distinguish their gender—just like Elizabeth prefers to be called Liz. Just like Elizabeth preferring to be called Liz, simply marking this in your grade book or class roster reminds you always to call on them using the name they have asked to be called, showing respect to the student.

This can also help substitute teachers, paraprofessionals, and others who may use your roll call sheet.

(Transgender-friendly policies in this book will discuss what that means, how to create them, and what to do if others in your school are less welcoming.)

As we move forward in this book, there may be situations that feel unrealistic because the people in your community are not inclusive, or those who explore related decisions are not inclusive. You are not being asked to go directly against what your supervisors say, but nothing prevents you from being someone who is aware of the knowledge and science related to the LGBT+ community. Nothing prevents you from being someone who is welcoming, and nothing prevents you from letting your students know that homophobic, biphobic, and transphobic language is never okay in your classroom.

6

Coming Out

What does "coming out" or "coming out of the closet" mean? It is the process of telling another person that you are LGBT+. There has been talk for decades about famous people coming out. Celebrities do it on the covers of magazines, singers do it at concerts or via their music videos, and some social media stars post entire videos of themselves coming out to their loved ones. In many areas of the country, the expectation is that of an immediate happy moment; an LGBT+ person hesitantly and fearfully tells someone they care about, and the person immediately embraces them and talks about how love knows no limits. In fact, it can be seen as homophobic/biphobic/transphobic if the person reacts any other way. While there is a lot to unpack in terms of the coming-out experience within families, let's focus on the experience and its importance within a school setting.

Students

When a student comes out at any age, they are choosing to let their peers and the school know something very personal about them. If a student comes out to you, this can be a surprise, and that surprise can lead to an uncomfortable or awkward interaction. As such, it can be better for educators and staff to think through the process generally, so they are at least somewhat prepared when the situation occurs in the future.

It is important to keep the focus on the student. Your personal thoughts, feelings, or opinions about LGBT+ people, coming out, or that student are not relevant in that moment. Instead, be mindful that the student is trusting you with information that speaks to their identity. Children of all ages in K–12 schools are growing and developing into future adults, and their sense of self and sense of self-worth is very malleable at this time. Your reaction and response can help or hinder their mental health and their self-confidence. As such, you may choose to thank them for sharing this. If the youth is coming out as a different gender, it may be appropriate to ask them if they would like you to call them by another name or use different pronouns. You might also wish to let them know that you accept them and that they can come to you any time they are in need of support.

You may want to inquire into who else knows. Here, you may glean information about whether the news is common knowledge among their peers, whether they have chosen to share this information with other adults, and how their home life is going. Remember that, unless there is a safety concern, it is never your place or your right to share this information with others. This is not a silly personality quirk that is fair game to joke about with the student; this is not gossip for the break room; this is not a topic to discuss at parent–teacher conferences. Student safety and privacy must be a priority, especially in a situation where sharing this information can lead to discrimination, bullying, or self-harm. If you think the student may be at risk of being harmed or harming themselves, follow standard safety protocols. However, be sure to find out beforehand whether the adults who are involved in these protocols are affirming and accepting. You want to guide the student to get the help they need; you do not want to refer them to someone who will further the problem. If you find that there is no one in that position to refer the student to, reach out to a state or national hotline for LGBT+ issues, and they can guide you toward the best option for student safety in this situation.

Allow the student to guide the conversation and to end it when they feel they are done sharing. You can periodically check in with them privately and keep an extra eye out for any slip in their grades or negative comments from peers. However, your treatment of the student should otherwise not change from before they came out to you. The goal is not to treat them as either less or more than their peers; it is simply to ensure their safety and to be an affirming person for them within the school.

School staff

Although it is common for the assumption to be that coming out is a stressor only for developing youth whose peers can be rude or downright cruel, the coming-out experience for adults can also be stressful. Coming out to a work colleague can be even more anxiety-inducing. This is because, in many cities and states, it is absolutely legal to be fired for being LGBT+. While there are currently federal laws protecting against discrimination for a person's race, age, or other traits, there is not yet such protection for LGBT+ people. (Some cities and states have created their own, so look into the laws in your area for specifics!) Even in places where there may be legal protections, letting a coworker know something personal can feel like opening the door to be judged, ridiculed, or mistreated. It is vital that you respond with kindness and support.

Let the staff member know that you value them, and you appreciate their choice to trust you with this information. If they are alerting you to a difference in gender identity, ask if they would like you to call them by another name or to use different pronouns. You can also ask for additional guidance on how you can best support them. Just as with students coming out, this information is highly personal and should never be discussed with others unless a safety concern is present. If there is such a concern, find out the protocol set up by your school. In many cases, there is an employee assistance program hotline you can call with questions. Be sure to keep the colleague's name anonymous while researching how to help, in order to protect their privacy. Just as with a student situation, if you are unsure whether a referral is to someone accepting, reach out to a state or federal LGBT+ help hotline for guidance.

7

Research Your Resources

In most school settings, there is a general awareness among staff regarding community resources. For example, if a student or staff member becomes combative or violent, the police are called. If there is an injury beyond the purview of the school nurse, the paramedics are called, and the person is taken to the hospital. If a child is being neglected or mistreated, they are turned over to Child Protective Services, and if they are in need of a home or food, they are referred to local homeless shelters, food pantries, and donation services. Sounds familiar, right?

But what if those referrals exacerbate the problem or put the person at higher risk of injury or mistreatment?

Safety and medical emergencies on school grounds

As you continue through the process of becoming more aware of the needs of LGBT+ people in your school community, take the time to research the organizations and resources that are commonly utilized (or even mandated by protocol). Find out whether the police and paramedics have been trained to treat LGBT+ people and, if they say they are, ask for information about what that training entails and whether it is mandated to everyone. Reach out to the local hospital or hospitals and find out about their policies and training programs for LGBT+ patients and families. Ask about specific support offered and skills training for this specific population. In addition, consider what information these professionals would request or require from the school in the event of an emergency situation. Are your school records up to date? How quickly are they changed to include gender identity or name changes, as needed? What are your school's rules on how much information is provided, and what are considered protected details of a student or staff member's life?

Health and wellness concerns at home

Over your years or decades working in schools, it is likely that you will encounter many students whose families are struggling financially. This may occur for a variety of reasons that are incredibly common. It may also occur if an adult in the family is LGBT+ identified, as this population is consistently underpaid and struggles to find and maintain employment in areas where discrimination against LGBT+ people remains legal. Regardless of what causes a family not to have enough money to cover all of their living expenses, these situations do happen. As such, you are likely to encounter situations where a family may be or become homeless and/or food-insecure. They may need assistance in purchasing school supplies and clothing. It is likely that your school already has a document prepared with a list of local homeless shelters, food pantries, and thrift or free stores. However, not every organization is accepting and affirming of LGBT+ people. Some use their religious affiliation as the reason they are not accepting. Others claim to have values that are based on their founder's upbringing many generations ago. Whatever the reasoning, it is not helpful to the family to refer them somewhere where they will be ridiculed and/or turned away when they are most in need of support.

Take the time to review and research the locations on the existing list. Look into the overarching organizations that fund or sponsor each program. Seek out information about how families are kept together in homeless shelters and whether this changes if the family has same-sex parents or a transgender person in their family unit. Find out whether the organizations' mission statements include religion of any sort and, if so, contact them to inquire about how staff and volunteers are trained to interact with LGBT+ people. You may find that there is little or no guidance given, allowing each worker to decide whether to welcome a family in or whether to turn them away for somehow living a life that goes against the organization's expectations or beliefs.

In some cases, schools may have a facility or community group that gathers neighbors and community leaders to put together care packages for families who cannot afford many basic items that children need.

These can be a great way to bring folks together and provide a sense of support and care within the community. However, you may also need to inquire into the practices and protocols of these groups as well as other local or federal organizations that donate holiday toys, school supplies, or clothing in regard to how they proceed when a child's gender identity is not aligned with their gender assigned at birth. Some may allow the family to identify the child's gender and use only that to pick out gifts, school materials, and outfits to give. Others may utilize school or birth records and refuse to deviate. In either situation, items that are gender-normative (all pink for girls, all blue for boys) may not be a fit for many of the youth in your school, and this may be a conversation to have with the organization for overarching reasons, not just for students who identify as a gender minority.

Safety emergencies occurring at home

In addition to emergency situations within the school and difficult times at home, LGBT+ youth may become unsafe at home due to their sexual and/or gender identity. This may result in physical, emotional, psychological, or even sexual abuse. It may result in significant neglect of the child's basic needs. Sometimes this is rooted in a parent or guardian's anger about the situation. Sometimes it is a misguided attempt to change the child into something more acceptable to the parent or guardian. You may see physical damage or begin to see the student's grades slip or their behavior change, or they may begin to attend school disheveled or appearing to be malnourished or unwashed. In most career or job training programs for positions within schools, the recommendation is to contact Child Protective Services. The intention is to have the department investigate the child's home life and remove the child from the home, if necessary, placing them into a foster care or group home situation.

However, many of these places are incredibly unsafe for LGBT+ youth. In some cases, if the child is not removed from the home, the parent/guardian becomes enraged that the student has gotten a government agency involved, which can amplify the abuse or neglect already occurring while also possibly removing them from the school district and the consistency of the school environment. This not only takes them from their family, but it also takes them away from friends, teachers, and you, someone who is affirming and supportive of their identity. This can be incredibly traumatic for a child. Plus, if the child is removed from the home, they may be placed in a home environment somewhere where they are bullied for their sexual orientation. It is also very likely that if they identify as a gender inconsistent with their assigned gender at birth, they will be placed in a same-sex group environment based on their birth gender. This can put the child at an increased risk of violence by others in the facility. This can lead the child to run away in an attempt to remove themselves from the violence. With nowhere to go, no money, no education, and no means to obtain a proper job, many of these runaways end up making choices based on the need for survival or to stop their minds from continuing to think about their current situation. This can lead to sexual behaviors in exchange for food, money, and/or somewhere to sleep for a night. It can lead to alcohol and/or drug use and abuse. Over time, this can lead to sexual assault, rape, self-harm, suicide attempts, or being murdered.

Rather than expect or assume that the Child Protective Services in your community is already trained and has the resources to be able to place an LGBT+ youth in an affirming environment, find out in advance of a situation. Contact the department to inquire about whether there are specific protocols for this youth population. Find out the details. If there are not, spend some time researching alternative options in your area.

The goal is simply to be prepared for an LGBT+ student or family in need so that you are ready to act at the time the need arises, rather than trying to juggle the emergent situation and completing research to ensure their safety as you transfer or refer them to the care of others.

Scenarios: Test Your Knowledge

Section summary

In this section, you will find scenarios that do happen, have happened, and are happening in K–12 schools across America. For each, you will find a scenario situation, thought questions, and guidance.

How to use this section

This section can be utilized individually or collectively. If you are reading this on your own, read the scenario, take time to answer each question in your mind or on paper, and then turn the page to find out how your responses fit with the guidance by the expert, as if she was on-call to guide you through this. Then, you'll see suggested readings at the back of the book. This will allow you to imagine the potential results, receive guidance from the expert, and to find out what research indicates, or what peer-reviewed publications would be useful to buttress the situation if you were to present the scenario and the guidance to your school in order to create or update policies. If you are reading this as a group, the scenario can be read aloud and the questions answered collectively; or the scenarios can be assigned to different breakout groups for consideration, discussion, and sharing with the larger group.

Section take-away

The purpose of this section is to imagine and examine what would happen if the provided scenario situation occurred in your own school, and to become more thoughtful about the various ways of handling each situation.

Scenario 1

A female student in your class named Jessica has just come up to you before school and asked to speak with you privately. She discloses that she is transgender. She asks that you call her James and that you use male pronouns both privately and during class. You have never had a transgender student before and are uncertain how to proceed.

1. If you were the sole decision-maker at your school, how would you choose for your school to handle this situation?

2. Based on what you know of those in decision-making positions at your school, what decision do you think they would make about how you must handle this situation?

3. Utilizing only your school's student handbook and staff handbook, what (if anything) do they dictate about how you must handle this situation?

4. If the answer to question #1 is different from the answers to question #2 and/or question #3, what can you do, in your role in the school? What (if anything) should you do?

SCENARIO 1.1

In addition to the information provided in Scenario 1, this conversation happens on Monday morning. That evening is parent–teacher conferences. You are scheduled to meet with this student's parent(s). This student discloses to you that their parents do not know about them being transgender and asks that you not tell them.

1. If you were the sole decision-maker at your school, how would you choose for your school to handle this situation?

2. Based on what you know of those in decision-making positions at your school, what decision do you think they would make about how you must handle this situation?

3. Utilizing only your school's student handbook and staff handbook, what (if anything) do they dictate about how you must handle this situation?

4. If the answer to question #1 is different from the answers to question #2 and/or question #3, what can you do, in your role in the school? What (if anything) should you do?

SCENARIO 1.2

In addition to the information provided in Scenario 1, the student discloses to you that their parents know about them being transgender, and they are "not at all okay with this." At the moment the student makes this statement, the bell rings, and other students begin entering your classroom. There is no time for further conversation with the student without others overhearing.

1. If you were the sole decision-maker at your school, how would you choose for your school to handle this situation?

2. Based on what you know of those in decision-making positions at your school, what decision do you think they would make about how you must handle this situation?

3. Utilizing only your school's student handbook and staff handbook, what (if anything) do they dictate about how you must handle this situation?

4. If the answer to question #1 is different from the answers to question #2 and/or question #3, what can you do, in your role in the school? What (if anything) should you do?

GUIDANCE

First, pat yourself on the back! This student feels safe enough to share this with you, which means you are doing a great job modeling what it looks like when an adult is trustworthy. Next, get more information from this student. Has James told all of his instructors? Will James be telling his classmates or just letting them figure it out when he is called on in class by a different name? Does his family know? How does James want you to handle each of those situations if not everyone knows? Also, ask about James' emotions and consider his safety. Does James feel safe at school and at home? Have you noticed James' grades slipping or him appearing to be struggling with anxiety or depression?

Now that you've gathered the facts, change all of your written records to reflect what James has told you. Make sure that the documents you use for grading, for assigning group work, etc. all say "James." If you have a packet for a substitute teacher, make sure to make a note in that packet, too. You may also want to include a note so that the substitute understands that James is transgender, not someone playing a joke on a substitute during roll call. This helps to ensure that James is called on appropriately. If you utilize computers or if anything is hung up in your classroom with student names, change the name to James. This will allow James to continue to be in the classroom as himself, without having to log into a computer program using the name he does not use or seeing items on the wall with a name that is no longer his name.

As for Scenario 1.1, find out what the school policy is when it comes to student privacy. If there is not a specific protocol for LGBT+ students, find out who to talk with about creating one and ask to contribute as, after reading this book, you'll be in a great position to advocate for inclusive policies! At this moment, though, it is about James and about the upcoming conference with James' parents. Remember that the first priority is always safety. Since James' parents do not know, and you don't know whether there is a safety risk, do not share this information. Since you have been asked not to tell them, this is actually going to be easy; you'll simply talk with them about their daughter the way you would have just before you had this conversation with James! (Wait to change James' name on any classroom materials until after the conference, too.) If you have noticed grade changes or depression, let the parents know that you are seeing this and suggest that they consider whether their child may benefit from speaking with a mental health professional. This can help to keep this student safe and get them to a therapist who can help them. (If, however, you live in an area that is very anti-LGBT+ or promotes conversion camps, you may not wish to refer the student out. In this case, you can offer James the number of a suicide prevention hotline or the Trevor Project Lifeline so he can gain support from professionals who are understanding and accepting of his identity). Continue to check in regularly with James.

When considering Scenario 1.2, this requires more information. Ask to see this student after class and ask if this means that he does not feel safe at home. If there is threat or experience of physical or emotional violence, proceed following the school's mandated protocol for child abuse. If you live in an area that is very anti-LGBT+ or promotes conversion camps, offer James the number of a suicide prevention hotline or the Trevor Project Lifeline so he can gain support from professionals who are understanding and accepting of his identity. Continue to check in regularly with James.

Scenario 2

You are a teacher in the physical education department or a sports coach who is well liked in your school. As such, you often hear gossip about students in the school from the students you most frequently interact with. You have just heard that one of your students is gay. This student participates in your gym class or on your sports team. This means that this student will be changing out of school clothes and into other attire in the locker room with other students of the same gender. You are not certain whether the student's sexuality is widely known throughout the school. You are unsure how other students feel about changing clothes in the locker room with someone who is attracted to the same gender.

1. If you were the sole decision-maker at your school, how would you choose for your school to handle this situation?

2. Based on what you know of those in decision-making positions at your school, what decision do you think they would make about how you must handle this situation?

3. Utilizing only your school's student handbook and staff handbook, what (if anything) do they dictate about how you must handle this situation?

4. If the answer to question #1 is different from the answers to question #2 and/or question #3, what can you do, in your role in the school? What (if anything) should you do?

GUIDANCE

There are a lot of details in this scenario, so let's break this down into what we know for sure, removing all of the things that may be rumors, misunderstandings, or inaccuracies. When we pare this down, all we know for sure is that there are students who think that one of your students is gay. Before we consider anything else, the feelings of fear that others are uncomfortable with a person because they are gay indicates outdated beliefs that someone's sexuality inherently makes them less safe to be around. It also indicates that there may be a misperception that a person's being gay makes them deserve to be sexualized. It is important that you take time to consider this belief within yourself, both to change the mistaken thinking and so your inherent bias does not become foundational for students.

In addition, when considering whether this bias may be existing for others, it is unknown whether the student is gay, whether others are correct in their assumptions, and whether anyone cares. That is all separate from anything having to do with the locker room situation. With this in mind, your best bet is to simply check in with the student in question. Since you do not know anything for sure about the student's sexuality and they have not addressed it with you, a general check-in is your best approach. The intention is not to try to find out if the rumors are true or to get the student to come out to you (if they are gay), but to ask how the student is doing. Does the student feel safe in the locker room? Are they being treated differently than their peers? Ask this in a space that is private enough for the student to feel able to speak freely while being mindful of your school's policies on one-on-one conversations. (For example, many schools require that student–teacher conversations occur in a place with a window or have the door open to prevent impropriety or the appearance of impropriety.)

If, after checking in with this student, you feel that they may be struggling, follow the school's protocol for working with a student who is struggling for any reason. This may involve including the guidance counselor, for example. Since this may be related to the student's sexuality, talk with the guidance counselor or school social worker.

Now that we've got a plan for the student, let's look at the locker room situation. We don't know right now whether there are any concerns by anyone about this specific student. However, this is a good time to check policies and procedures about how this would be handled in the event that this scenario occurred, and it was a problem. If there is a plan in place, know what it is and consider, after reading this book, whether this is the most inclusive policy. If it is, awesome! We can move on! If not, find out who to discuss this with and how to work with them to create an improved policy that is inclusive. If there is no policy at all, ask the policy-maker at your school if they would allow you to write that policy. If they will (or if they will allow you to write it with them), this would be a great time to create the most inclusive policy possible.

What might that look like? First, tie it into the existing anti-bullying policies. It is fairly standard that school policies state that bullying is not permitted for any reason at any time anywhere on school grounds. Thus this would include locker room bullying. Next, consider the unique nature of an LGBT+ student. Consider that they may be struggling with their bodies or that others may be judgmental of the locker room experience based on a student's LGBT+ identity. Now, think about what other groups this may be true for. This could include people with disabilities, those with anxiety, students with trauma due to abuse, and students who may simply not feel confident in their bodies. Suddenly, this policy stops being "just about LGBT+ students" and now becomes a policy about many students. (This makes it tougher for the administration to refuse.) Perhaps your locker room allows for curtains or stalls to be installed, so students have access to private changing areas. If not (or if there are not enough), is there a nearby restroom that students can use for added privacy?

If this is for a physical education class, perhaps reconsider why a change of clothes is required. Could the policy be changed so that students are simply required to wear clothing and shoes in which they can move around freely? This would allow students to choose to dress for school wearing pants and sneakers, if they chose, preventing them from needing to change at all, which could also eliminate some of the problems with locker room anxiety and stress.

If this is for a sports team where a uniform is required, offering options for different changing areas, staggered start times so there are fewer students changing at a time, or having a staff member within earshot of the locker room so that any bullying would be heard and interrupted could all work well to eliminate some of the problems with locker room anxiety and stress.

Scenario 3

You are a teacher in your school district's high school. In addition, you are the advisor to the department that oversees everything related to the students' annual prom. This includes Prom King and Prom Queen nominations and voting, and announcing the winners. The school policy dictates that students can nominate anyone for these roles and that the top three people nominated in each category are voted on. Your role is to count the ballots after voting and to announce the winner over the PA system at the end of the school day. After the students have finished voting, you have begun to count the votes in your classroom. You discover that the winners of Prom King and Prom Queen are a same-sex couple. This has never happened before, and you are unsure of how to proceed. You know that students are expecting to hear who won at the end of the school day, approximately six hours from now.

1. If you were the sole decision-maker at your school, how would you choose for your school to handle this situation?

2. Based on what you know of those in decision-making positions at your school, what decision do you think they would make about how you must handle this situation?

3. Utilizing only your school's student handbook and staff handbook, what (if anything) do they dictate about how you must handle this situation?

4. If the answer to question #1 is different from the answers to question #2 and/or question #3, what can you do, in your role in the school? What (if anything) should you do?

GUIDANCE

While you are new to this situation, it is unknown whether there is already a policy in place. First, find out. It may be that this is the first time this has ever happened. If it is, you can choose to name the winners as you always have and let the school choose whether/how to respond. If you think your school may not be accepting of this action, you may choose to speak with the person who used to hold this role or ask your supervisor to find out if this has happened, how it was handled, and whether there is a policy in place for this situation. If there is, is the policy inclusive? If it is not, are you able to alter the policy to make it more inclusive within the short time you have? It is possible that there is no policy to contend with and you can simply announce the winners as they were voted on by the students and it will be treated the same as every other year's winners.

You may discover that your school is not inclusive and accepting of the same-sex couple winning. With this knowledge, you may be forced to choose whether to announce no winners, announce the second-place winner(s), or announce the winners, knowing you may upset your supervisor. You may be given direct instructions from your superior about how to proceed. If the instructions do not support inclusivity, you'll need to treat this situation as you would any other in which you strongly disagree with your supervisor. Is there another supervisor to speak with? Is there a protocol in place for situations where disagreement occurs? Are you willing to risk the consequences of not following orders? You may choose to announce that the counting will be completed within the next few days and the winners will be announced soon. This will upset the students but allow you more time to talk with stakeholders on how to proceed in the most inclusive way. You may choose to defy orders and announce the winners as they were voted, knowing that there may be consequences for this choice. Before making any decision, it may be beneficial to speak with a seasoned colleague whom you trust, any significant other you may have who might be impacted by any consequences, and if you are part of a teachers' union, you may want to contact them for guidance.

Scenario 4

It is the end of summer break and, just as it happens every year, you and the rest of the school's faculty are coming into the school for mandatory staff sessions in preparation for the upcoming school year. Upon entering the auditorium, you spot Mr. Johnson, one of the school's eldest and most beloved teachers. As you begin to approach him to say hello, you notice he is wearing pants, a blouse, and heels. When he turns around to greet you, you notice he is wearing lipstick. He notices your surprise and tells you that, over the summer, he came out to his family, and he will begin this school year, "finally getting to be called Mrs. Johnson." You are unsure whether the administration or other staff know about this.

1. If you were the sole decision-maker at your school, how would you choose for your school to handle this situation?

2. Based on what you know of those in decision-making positions at your school, what decision do you think they would make about how you must handle this situation?

3. Utilizing only your school's student handbook and staff handbook, what (if anything) do they dictate about how you must handle this situation?

4. If the answer to question #1 is different from the answers to question #2 and/or question #3, what can you do, in your role in the school? What (if anything) should you do?

GUIDANCE

There are three things happening simultaneously here: your surprise, their happiness about their open identity as Mrs. Johnson, and your wondering if others know about this. Let's start with that last one. Since you're coming into a meeting for all staff, whether others already know about this or are about to be surprised by this doesn't much matter, because soon the room will fill up and everyone will know. Since the lipstick and the introduction as Mrs. Johnson clued you in, they will likely do the same as others enter the room. So there's no need to wonder, worry, or concern yourself with what others know. You don't even need to worry about you knowing what others do not, as Mrs. Johnson is not only choosing to wear a shade of lipstick that is obvious, but she is also openly talking about herself as Mrs. Johnson—and she is making a point of saying how happy she is about being Mrs. Johnson.

This just leaves your surprise and Mrs. Johnson's happiness about openly being Mrs. Johnson. While your surprise will dissipate as the new information becomes information you've known for longer and longer, what stands is Mrs. Johnson's happiness about openly being Mrs. Johnson. You can also presume that this new information may cause some comments and conversations from your peers. Mrs. Johnson isn't a fool; it is certain she knows this will probably happen, and she has likely spent days, weeks, months, or even years preparing herself for them. However, you do not need to leave her to brave that on her own. How supportive do you want to be right now?

You have three options. In order of least brave to most brave: stand or sit in the room in silence while the others in the room discuss this new information; stand or sit next to Mrs. Johnson and offer comments of support, knowing she is overhearing whatever may be being said about her; or roam the room, listening for others to talk about this and jumping in to either share words of support for Mrs. Johnson or shut down negative commentary.

While the bravest option may be tied to your seniority at the meeting or your knowledge and relationships with your peers, it also offers you the strongest opportunity to advocate and support someone who is in a vulnerable position in the room. Plus, since Mrs. Johnson has significant seniority, you would be buttressing on that while supporting her; if that does not feel like something that you can do, for whatever reason, sitting with Mrs. Johnson both to offer her words of support and to visually show solidarity can send a strong message to your peers about your beliefs concerning inclusion in schools.

Let's say, though, that, at the moment, you weren't sure what to do so you just sat down for the meeting, saying nothing and doing nothing regarding Mrs. Johnson. Now you're reading this, rethinking that moment, and wishing you would have done things differently. Whether that meeting was yesterday, last school year, or a decade ago, reach out to Mrs. Johnson now! Apologize to her for missing the opportunity to support her more directly. Ask her what you can do for her now to support her. If she has already retired, take time to think about and create a plan for the next Mrs. Johnson (whether this would be a staff member or a student). Decide how you will show your support when that person comes out to the school as transgender. Then, when the moment happens, follow through. (You might even consider sending a letter to Mrs. Johnson to tell her how knowing her inspired you to act differently in the next situation.)

Scenario 5

On Friday after school hours, the federal government signed a bill into law that discriminates against LGBT+ people. You know that there are students and staff at your school who openly identify as LGBT+ and that there are students and staff who have LGBT+ loved ones. It is Monday morning, and you are commuting to school. You know that the new law will be brought up at school both by students and by staff, as it is considered to be major news.

1. If you were the sole decision-maker at your school, how would you choose for your school to handle this situation?

2. Based on what you know of those in decision-making positions at your school, what decision do you think they would make about how you must handle this situation?

3. Utilizing only your school's student handbook and staff handbook, what (if anything) do they dictate about how you must handle this situation?

4. If the answer to question #1 is different from the answers to question #2 and/or question #3, what can you do, in your role in the school? What (if anything) should you do?

SCENARIO 5.1

How might this be different if the decision was made by your state's government?

SCENARIO 5.2

How might this be different if the decision was made by your local community's government?

GUIDANCE

This is a great opportunity for conversations about the way laws get made. Although this may seem best left to the history teacher and you may teach another subject, allow this to lead to discussions about how federal laws impact people. Guide students through discussions about the importance of researching candidates and voting. Give students space to share their frustrations and to talk about how they may feel helpless since they are not old enough to vote. Ask them to brainstorm ideas about how to let current politicians know how they feel about this decision and how they can influence the adults in their lives who can vote.

For Scenario 5.1, continue the conversation but also offer the opportunity for your students to find out about state-wide opportunities to speak with the politicians in your state. Encourage them to research the politicians making state-wide decisions and to find out how to be in contact with them to discuss their beliefs and how they want to encourage these state representatives to vote. This may include attending age- or issue-based lobby days, it may focus on attending town hall meetings when the politician is in their area, or it may be an opportunity for the students to come together to work on requesting a visit by one or more politicians. Guiding them to do the research and to do the work not only helps them toward their goal but also encourages their activism and their sense of community as they work together to find ways to reach out to their own representatives.

Scenario 5.2 can also be responded to in this way, though the local aspect may offer even more opportunity for students to speak up about their concerns and their emotions. Some may have personal ties to one or more decision-maker. It may become easier to encourage one of the decision-makers to visit the school to speak with students. It may be impactful for students to individually or collectively write a letter to be published in the local newspaper. Television news may be interested in a story talking with students as they speak out. As students explore avenues to publicize their opinion, be sure to remind them that, as minors, they may require parental permission in order to be publicizing their names and faces.

In addition, no matter which scenario is most accurate for the situation, be sure to offer students continual age-appropriate opportunities to remain aware of situations before votes or changes occur so they can work to encourage what they believe or prevent voting on a particular issue from occurring, rather than to always being in a reactive role. This can be done in unison as a school, in concert with your colleagues who may teach history, writing, and other directly related classes, or as an ongoing topic within your own classroom. Talking with your colleagues may guide you in how to proceed.

Scenario 6

On your way out of school yesterday, you walked past a student, Jamie, who was holding hands with another student of the same gender. This surprised you, but you said nothing. This morning, the student approached you. Jamie says, "So I know you saw me yesterday holding hands with Mickey. Please, please don't tell my parents. They'd kill me if they found out I'm bi." Just as the student finishes this sentence, another student approaches you with a question about an upcoming field trip. By the time you turn back to Jamie, they have walked away. Later that day, you receive an email from Jamie's parent. In the email, the parent asks for your help. They say, "Jamie has been acting strange at home. We don't know what's going on. We thought you might have some idea."

1. If you were the sole decision-maker at your school, how would you choose for your school to handle this situation?

2. Based on what you know of those in decision-making positions at your school, what decision do you think they would make about how you must handle this situation?

3. Utilizing only your school's student handbook and staff handbook, what (if anything) do they dictate about how you must handle this situation?

4. If the answer to question #1 is different from the answers to question #2 and/or question #3, what can you do, in your role in the school? What (if anything) should you do?

SCENARIO 6.1

Would your answers to the questions change if Jamie was 8 years old? If so, how? If not, why not?

SCENARIO 6.2

Would your answers to the questions change if Jamie was 12 years old? If so, how? If not, why not?

SCENARIO 6.3

Would your answers to the questions change if Jamie was 18 years old? If so, how? If not, why not?

GUIDANCE

When reading this scenario as a whole, it can be easy to connect Jamie holding hands and identifying to you as bisexual to the email from their parent. However, that connection is unknown at this point. Before assuming a link, it would be fair to respond to Jamie's parent and ask for more information. This may tell you whether the concern is about something completely different. If the concern is different, respond as you would have before seeing Jamie holding hands with anyone; focus on the parental concerns, and work with the parent to find a solution, whether this is via connecting them to school resources or reassuring the parent. If the concern is clearly tied to Jamie's sexuality and their work to hide it from their parent(s), ask to speak with Jamie. Have a private conversation where Jamie can speak freely, but be sure to follow school protocols on how teacher–student privacy can occur so that there is no appearance of impropriety. Explain to Jamie that you received an email from their concerned parent and ask for more information about whether the home is safe for Jamie.

If there is a safety concern, follow school protocol to report this. If the safety concern is unknown because Jamie is assuming that home will become unsafe if they come out as bisexual, offer to help Jamie. Follow school protocols for this, if they exist. If they do not, talk with decision-makers about being on the team to create a protocol so that the written rule can be as inclusive as possible. In the meantime, let Jamie know that you are working to support them and that, as such, you'd like to discuss this with the school social worker or guidance counselor. If Jamie refuses, ask what adult(s) they feel comfortable with you discussing this with. Invite them to go with you to talk with these adults. Let Jamie know that, for safety reasons, you cannot simply do nothing, so your goal is to work together to find a solution. Be sure you are documenting everything as this conversation is occurring. If you decide to seek out external resources to guide you, such as the Trevor Project Lifeline or a local LGBT+ organization, maintain school privacy protocols at all times. Work together within the parameters of your role and bring in those with more experience in home-life trauma and mental healthcare to encourage and support Jamie through offering honesty to their parent(s) while also having a safety plan in case home becomes unsafe or in case Jamie's fear of coming out causes them to behave in a way that is not safe.

In Scenarios 6.1 and 6.2, this guidance stands. You may also wish to offer the student the opportunity to speak via phone with someone at an LGBT+ support hotline, with an adult in the room, during the school day. This may allow guidance and access to support that the student might not feel safe contacting from home or via a cell phone their parent pays for and can review the bill for.

In Scenario 6.3, review the school protocol and the state laws about school privacy when a student is legally an adult. If protocols and laws support a student being seen as a legal child until graduation, previous guidance applies. If the school and state see the student as an adult, let the student know you received a concerned email from their parent. Respond to the parent's email explaining that your ability to discuss Jamie with them is limited due to Jamie's adult status and offer them contact information for the school counselor if they would like to request a family meeting, knowing that Jamie can legally decline to participate or attend.

Scenario 7

As part of your school's mandated curriculum, health class is included in every student's schedule. This includes information about physical anatomy, sexual behaviors, and sexually transmitted infections, using age-appropriate language. You discover that the book used for class and the lesson plans provided by the book publisher only include cisgender bodies and heterosexual relationships. While you do not know the sexual orientations and gender identities of every student and staff member, you know that there are LGBT+ parents whose children attend the school.

1. If you were the sole decision-maker at your school, how would you choose for your school to handle this situation?

2. Based on what you know of those in decision-making positions at your school, what decision do you think they would make about how you must handle this situation?

3. Utilizing only your school's student handbook and staff handbook, what (if anything) do they dictate about how you must handle this situation?

4. If the answer to question #1 is different from the answers to question #2 and/or question #3, what can you do, in your role in the school? What (if anything) should you do?

SCENARIO 7.1 _____

Would your answers to the questions change if the class was being taught in elementary school? If so, how? If not, why not?

SCENARIO 7.2 _____

Would your answers to the questions change if the class was being taught in middle school? If so, how? If not, why not?

SCENARIO 7.3

Would your answers to the questions change if the class was being taught in high school? If so, how? If not, why not?

SCENARIO 7.4

Would your answers to the questions change if the class was being taught to high school seniors, all of whom would be 18 years old or turning 18 years old during the course term? If so, how? If not, why not?

GUIDANCE

This scenario may seem, on its surface, as a no-win situation. It's easy to picture everyone wanting something different, and you and your school are stuck in the middle, right? It doesn't have to be that way! First, look at the existing curriculum and book(s) used. Is it possible to make small additions to the materials to become more inclusive? For example, is it possible to turn a quiz about safe-sex behaviors into one without genders being used, swapping out "your partner" for gendered words? Is it possible to create a statement or additional handout to provide to students to articulate why gender and sexuality are being taught and to guide them toward recognizing inclusion and lack thereof as they read? This is likely the least disruptive method of correcting the problem.

However, this may not be enough, either based on what the book information gives or because you now know enough about LGBT+ people that you want to ensure that your students receive a more well-rounded education in this class. In this case, look at the answers to your questions for this scenario and use them to guide you through making these changes happen.

For Scenarios 7.1, 7.2, and 7.3, the biggest difference is the simplicity of the language being used and finding out whether your state or school district has requirements regarding parental notification before teaching specific materials. This will offer guidance in choosing words that are inclusive and at the level of your learners. A great example here would be to use Jazz Jennings' materials. At the elementary-school level, there is a book called *I Am Jazz*. The book discusses Jazz being a transgender girl who was born with a "girl brain and a boy body." At the middle-school level, she has an autobiographical book that would add to a student's understanding of the experience of a transgender teen called *Being Jazz: My Life as a (Transgender) Teen*. At the high-school level, it would be age-appropriate for students to watch episodes or the entirety of her television series, *I Am Jazz*, which chronicles Jazz's high school years and her move through graduation and into college. Not only could any of these resources be used individually, but a school district could also decide to work together to utilize all of these platforms and effectively let their students grow up with Jazz and her story. This offers a perspective of the transgender identity through the lens of a person their own age, using life experiences and developmental milestones that are age-appropriate both to Jazz and to the students engaging in Jazz's story.

As for Scenario 7.4, there may be no difference between this scenario and Scenarios 7.1–7.3, depending on your school district policies. In some schools, permission slips for parental approval are no longer necessary once a student is 18 years old. If this is applicable in your school, you may be able to offer a class to students 18+ years old in which information can be shared that students would be interested to learn, but that may not easily pass parental approval. This may be worth considering if your students would be interested and if you would be willing to teach it. If so, you can talk with your administrators about how to create and gain class approval so it can be offered in an upcoming school term.

Scenario 8

You are in your current role within your current school. One of your students is openly gay. Recently, you assigned a group project, which is due in one week. You explained that the groups would likely need to meet via phone or in person after school to complete this assignment. The next day, you receive an email from the parent of one of the students. "I am writing because of the group project you assigned. I would like for my child, Chris, to be put in another group. In our household, we do not condone homosexuality. We do not want Chris to work in this group with the homosexual student. In addition, please ensure that Chris is never assigned to group or pairs work with this student and that they are never assigned seats next to each other."

1. If you were the sole decision-maker at your school, how would you choose for your school to handle this situation?

2. Based on what you know of those in decision-making positions at your school, what decision do you think they would make about how you must handle this situation?

3. Utilizing only your school's student handbook and staff handbook, what (if anything) do they dictate about how you must handle this situation?

4. If the answer to question #1 is different from the answers to question #2 and/or question #3, what can you do, in your role in the school? What (if anything) should you do?

SCENARIO 8.1

Would your answers to the questions be different if, instead of being openly gay, the student was openly transgender? If so, how? If not, why not?

SCENARIO 8.2 _____

Would your answers to the questions be different depending on the age or grade of the students? If so, at what ages would the answers change and how? If not, why not?

GUIDANCE

Depending on where you are, you may have already received an email like this or you may not be able to imagine anyone receiving an email like this; American school experiences vary so wildly! However, since people relocate all the time, no matter how open your student population typically is, a new student in your district may come from a place where sending this type of email to you seems logical and right for that family. When we remove all of the details, we come down to two options here: either reassign Chris to a different group and never put Chris and the gay classmate together, or refuse to condone Chris' parents' request and treat Chris, the gay class-mate, and all students the same and randomly assign them for group work, seating, etc., using the same methods for all students.

As a reader of this book, you've long figured out that the goal here is typically to enforce inclusion wherever possible and to remove stigma and ignorance. Chris would very likely benefit from interacting with many different types of people, as all students do. However, we do not know if Chris is upset or if keeping Chris in a group with a gay classmate would lead to Chris bullying the classmate. We would also need to know whether the school policies, city policies, or state laws have mandates against discrimination against sexual orientation. If so, it would make sense to pull Chris aside and discuss the situation. First hear Chris's thoughts and feelings on the subject, and if he agrees with his parents' concerns. Listen to Chris' concerns, talk with Chris about the non-bullying policies in school, and regularly check in with the group members individually and collectively to ensure a safe experience for everyone. This may also require you to include your supervisor, as sending a response to Chris' parents refusing to remove their child may create further tension or reaction by the parents. Your school may even wish to involve legal counsel simply to protect themselves.

In other schools, it is preferred to avoid conflict with parents and thus moving Chris would be school protocol. Even then, it would be a great idea to speak with Chris, so it is understood that Chris' parents requested the move, even if you decide to let the parents explain why they asked for Chris to be placed in a new group. You'll also want to be sure not to cause the group members to take on additional work because of this, as it would not be right for an entire group to suffer due to Chris' parents.

For Scenario 8.1, the guidance would not change unless the school's policy specifically considers gender identity the same as gender for non-discrimination purposes. In this case, follow the same protocols as above, letting the parents know that you would not be legally permitted to make the requested changes, nor would Chris be able to do so within the classroom.

In Scenario 8.2, the only possible change would be if Chris was 18+ years old. In this case, the parents may have no say at all in what happens with Chris in the classroom. If so, you could simply email to let them know that, due to Chris' age as a legal adult, any requests about the classroom or school-related concerns would need to come to you from Chris directly and that you cannot discuss Chris' schooling with them due to privacy laws. You could also then discuss the situation with Chris, offer education and guidance about sexuality to answer questions or dispel myths, and/or reinforce school policies on bullying, to ensure that Chris gains access to accurate information needed to proceed in class with gay classmates in a manner that is safe for everyone.

Scenario 9

While walking from the cafeteria to your classroom (or office), you overhear two students calling a third student names. As you approach, you hear that the names are based on the student's sexual orientation. Before you get close enough to say something, the three students see you and all run off in the other direction. Later, you see the third student alone in the hall. You ask if everything is okay. They respond, "I know you saw the whole thing earlier, but it's nothing. I mean, it's not *nothing*, but it's no big deal. Just don't say anything, okay? Because if you say something, they'll think I said something and then it'll be way worse."

1. If you were the sole decision-maker at your school, how would you choose for your school to handle this situation?

2. Based on what you know of those in decision-making positions at your school, what decision do you think they would make about how you must handle this situation?

3. Utilizing only your school's student handbook and staff handbook, what (if anything) do they dictate about how you must handle this situation?

4. If the answer to question #1 is different from the answers to question #2 and/or question #3, what can you do, in your role in the school? What (if anything) should you do?

SCENARIO 9.1

Would your answers to the questions be different if, instead of the comments being about the student's sexual orientation, they were about the student's gender identity? If so, how? If not, why not?

SCENARIO 9.2

Would your answers to the questions be different depending on the age or grade of the students? If so, at what ages would the answers change and how? If not, why not?

GUIDANCE

For every scenario in this section, you will need to take into account your school and school district's bullying policies as well as any local, state, and federal laws that may protect against discrimination on the basis of sexual orientation and/or gender identity (or on gender in general). Although it is very common for victims of bullying to fear upsetting the bullies, you can point out to the student that you witnessed the situation firsthand and that this will be stated to the bullies, to help make it clear how you became aware of the situation. In addition, while following the protocol for handling bullying situations, it may be a good idea to include the guidance counselor or social worker to ensure that the student being bullied can be assessed for safety and offered resources.

The only situation in which age or grade may matter is if the bullying becomes a legal concern. If this occurs, the students' ages may alter the way they are charged with committing a crime, as well as what court they would be tried in and the severity of their sentence, if convicted. Parental involvement may also change due to age, both in terms of whether the parents can be held responsible legally and whether the parents are included in the school conversation about the situation. If the actions of a bully are at or nearing legal concerns, in addition to bringing in the guidance counselor or social worker, it may be wise to include your school's police or community officer in order to enlighten the student about the legal ramifications of bullying so that the student has access to all information while making future choices.

Scenario 10

Your school is preparing for Community Night, an evening in which the school is open to the public to see what students are learning, to view student artwork, to meet the school staff, and to explore the new taxpayer-funded computer lab. As such, everyone is hard at work beautifying the school. While walking down the hall, you realize that every poster promoting family support and togetherness depicts white families with a mother and a father. You know that there are members of the community in same-sex marriages and students in the school who are of other races.

1. If you were the sole decision-maker at your school, how would you choose for your school to handle this situation?

2. Based on what you know of those in decision-making positions at your school, what decision do you think they would make about how you must handle this situation?

3. Utilizing only your school's student handbook and staff handbook, what (if anything) do they dictate about how you must handle this situation?

4. If the answer to question #1 is different from the answers to question #2 and/or question #3, what can you do, in your role in the school? What (if anything) should you do?

5. If asked for feedback, what is an example of what you might say and who is the best person to have this conversation with?

GUIDANCE

First, yay for you for noticing something that has likely been going on all around you for years or even decades! You noticing this indicates a growth mindset that shows you are open to learning new ideas and that you are seeking ways to include all families and people in your school. We don't know how much time there is between this realization and Community Night to know if there is time or budget to purchase additional posters to add to the halls. If so, talking with the person who makes these purchases can be a great option to solve this problem. (Even if it's too late to receive new posters by this Community Night event, this conversation is a great one to have in order to prevent this concern for future Community Night events.)

What if there is no time to get new posters? How about involving extra-curricular groups or teachers' helpers? A quick gathering of poster board and/or using the school computers can lead students to create inclusive wall hangings quickly, and it lets them own the experience of thinking about how to make the space more inclusive to everyone who may come into their school. You can assign students to support specific minority groups or types of families as you see a need, or you can task them to think about what types of people are not being honored or acknowledged on the walls and to create their own ideas from there. (Be sure to have them create a rough draft on scratch paper before using supplies to create the final posters so that you can ensure accurate and appropriate wording and inclusion!)

Scenario 11

Recently, your student Jonathan has come out at school as transgender. Jonathan has now asked to be called Tiffany and to utilize female pronouns. During a staff meeting, a teacher keeps talking about this student, using male pronouns and calling the student "Jonathan." When you ask the teacher about this, the teacher rolls their eyes and says, "Oh, you mean, 'Tiffany'?" and uses air quotes.

1. If you were the sole decision-maker at your school, how would you choose for your school to handle this situation?

2. Based on what you know of those in decision-making positions at your school, what decision do you think they would make about how you must handle this situation?

3. Utilizing only your school's student handbook and staff handbook, what (if anything) do they dictate about how you must handle this situation?

4. If the answer to question #1 is different from the answers to question #2 and/or question #3, what can you do, in your role in the school? What (if anything) should you do?

SCENARIO 11.1

Would your answers to the questions be different depending on the age or grade of the students? If so, at what ages would the answers change and how? If not, why not?

SCENARIO 11.2

Would your answers be different if the student's parents had reached out to complain to you about the teacher refusing to use the student's correct name and pronouns? If so, how? If not, why not?

GUIDANCE

Having made it this far through this book, it is understandable that this teacher's behavior is giving you pause. (Yay for you for recognizing a problematic situation that may not have caught your attention before beginning this book! *high five*) However, we don't know what this teacher knows about gender or about transgender people, so we do not yet know whether this behavior is due to intentional misgendering and inappropriate behavior or someone who currently lacks the education necessary to understand what it means to have a transgender person in the school and to understand appropriate responses to Tiffany both in her presence and out of her presence. Based on this, try to approach this teacher privately. Explain that you weren't sure, based on their wording earlier, if they needed some support on the way to accepting Tiffany's name and gender pronouns.

(You can offer to share your copy of this book or recommend they purchase a copy. You can even offer to start a book club using this book and, later, other books on diversity.)

If the teacher refuses or if the conversation with the teacher indicates that the teacher is aware yet intentionally misgendering Tiffany, speak with your supervisor. The goal is not to get someone in trouble; it is to protect Tiffany and other students from being bullied by school staff. Before reporting this to your supervisor, you may first need to ascertain the supervisor's level of education and knowledge on gender and transgender people. You can offer the same guidance and support to them as you did to the teacher. The goal is to help guide and educate folks so that Tiffany and others are treated with respect, both by those who have gained an education and knowledge base and by those who recognize that not treating students appropriately will lead to career ramifications.

In Scenario 11.1, grades and ages only matter in regard to the age range of the specific research or teaching tools that you refer the educators you are helping to guide to. These may help the uneducated/undereducated to better understand gender identity at your student population's age range as well as how to answer the questions other students may ask you about the change in the student's name and pronouns.

Regarding Scenario 11.2, this indicates an ongoing problem that has become consistent enough that the student complained at home and that the parents are now reaching out. While you will need to follow your school's protocol of handling parental complaints about another staff member, you may wish to follow this situation more closely than more generalized complaints, as it may be necessary for school staff with gender education to advocate for the student and for inclusive policies and procedures. This can help prevent those without understanding from creating repercussions or school protocols that can lead to unintended negative impacts on gender minorities within the school. You can also provide support to the student while they are in school to ensure that they have a trusted adult in the building during the times in which they are in the care of the school.

Scenario 12

As usual, you've stayed long after the end of the school day to finish some work. On your way out of the school, you notice a student, Jordan, sitting outside. From the looks of it, it seems Jordan has been there for a number of hours. When you approach, Jordan seems sheepish and is non-committal when you ask how long they've been sitting there. You ask why Jordan hasn't gone home. Jordan says, "It's not that I hate going home, exactly, it's just that, when I'm at school, I can be me, ya know? When I'm home, I have to try to pretend to be someone I'm not." Confused, you ask what Jordan means. Jordan says, "My parents don't know I'm gay. If they ever found out, I'd be kicked out. Like right that second, 'here's the door, get out' kinda kicked out." You ask about relatives and Jordan tells you, "I don't have any living grandparents, and both of my parents are only children, so it's just the three of us. It isn't that I like hiding who I am from them, but I know for sure they'd kick me out, I know for sure I have nowhere else to go, and I know for sure I can't afford to live somewhere by myself. So I mostly hang out here at school as much as I can. Yeah, it means I don't really have dinner because I'm avoiding talking to my parents, but I just try to eat my own lunch and everything my friends don't eat from their lunches, which mostly keeps me full till school breakfast." When you ask about weekends, Jordan tells you, "Sometimes I go to a friend's house and conveniently it's right around mealtime. Other times, I just have to hang in there till breakfast at school on Monday. It's no big deal, though; I've been doing this for months, and I'm used to it."

1. If you were the sole decision-maker at your school, how would you choose for your school to handle this situation?

2. Based on what you know of those in decision-making positions at your school, what decision do you think they would make about how you must handle this situation?

3. Utilizing only your school's student handbook and staff handbook, what (if anything) do they dictate about how you must handle this situation?

4. If the answer to question #1 is different from the answers to question #2 and/or question #3, what can you do, in your role in the school? What (if anything) should you do?

SCENARIO 12.1

Would your answers to the questions be different depending on the age or grade of the students? If so, at what ages would the answers change and how? If not, why not?

SCENARIO 12.2

Would your answers to the questions be different if, instead of the situation being about the student's sexual orientation, it was about the student's gender identity? If so, how? If not, why not?

GUIDANCE

There are lots of details here so it can become easy to feel overwhelmed. When focusing only on the causes for concern, it comes down to Jordan telling you that there is a housing instability situation, which has led to a food instability situation. This breaks down into two separate timing categories: immediate and long-term. Immediately, Jordan is hungry, and it seems there will not be another meal until Jordan's school breakfast tomorrow. If you have food with you or if it does not break a school rule, offering to pick up some snacks or a meal for Jordan would not be odd. However, you would need to emphasize that this cannot be a daily situation. You can, however, let Jordan know that tomorrow, you will begin to work together to find a solution that does not involve Jordan living in fear of homelessness and going hungry on a regular basis. When you get home, document everything that was said and done in the situation, so you have the details for your records, and so you can provide the record to the school.

It would be very difficult to figure out whether Jordan is right about being kicked out if the parents found out about Jordan's sexuality, so that is not likely an option. As such, this means it is time to discuss the concern with the guidance counselor and any resources available at the school. There may also be options in the community, so discuss this within the school first to find out what the protocols are and to create a plan.

For Scenario 12.1, at any age, considering housing and food security and planning for Jordan's mental and physical safety are always the priority. However, Jordan's age and grade may matter. This is because it can determine the number of legal issues. First, depending on Jordan's age, allowing the child to be unsupervised and unaccounted for may be a crime of child neglect in your area. Second, an older child may have had some of the same friends long enough to be able to accurately assess whether any of their parents may be safe to come out to and stay with, in the event of an emergency housing situation. Finally, if Jordan is old enough, it may be possible, in an extreme need situation, to work to get Jordan emancipated and provided government assistance to be able to live independently while remaining in school. If Jordan is not old enough for emancipation consideration and lacks a safe place to go, you may need to complete additional research on the foster care system and homeless youth shelter situations for LGBT+ youth. Unfortunately, these more public spaces can be dangerous for LGBT+ youth and the goal is to get Jordan into a safe environment, not to remove him from a currently known (albeit not great) situation and into something much more dangerous.

Scenario 12.2 follows much of the same protocol as Scenario 12.1. However, homeless and foster situations are often divided by gender. This can make finding a safe placement for Jordan even more difficult. A plan may be needed to find a temporary situation while professionals seek out a longer-term placement option for Jordan to live. It is also vital that Jordan is regularly monitored to prevent harassment or violence in any temporary or long-term living environment and to ensure a safety plan for Jordan both to get away from an unsafe situation and to seek help if Jordan begins to consider self-harm.

Scenario 13

You are in charge of a classroom of students, and you ask them to pair off to complete an activity. As the students separate into pairs, you notice that one student, Jude, is being actively ignored by their peers. You decide to give the students a moment to see if they self-correct, moving closer to listen in on what they are saying to one another. You hear them say that they won't partner with Jude because Jude's mom is "weird." You do not know a lot about Jude's mom, but you've been told by a teacher in another classroom that Jude's mom is "somewhere on the LGBT+ spectrum."

1. If you were the sole decision-maker at your school, how would you choose for your school to handle this situation?

2. Based on what you know of those in decision-making positions at your school, what decision do you think they would make about how you must handle this situation?

3. Utilizing only your school's student handbook and staff handbook, what (if anything) do they dictate about how you must handle this situation?

4. If the answer to question #1 is different from the answers to question #2 and/or question #3, what can you do, in your role in the school? What (if anything) should you do?

SCENARIO 13.1

Would your answers to the questions be different depending on the age or grade of the students? If so, at what ages would the answers change and how? If not, why not?

GUIDANCE

Although the reasoning for Jude being ostracized is due to their mom being LGBT+, begin by treating this as you would any situation in which a student is being left out. If those methods do not work, remind students of the anti-bullying policies in your school. Make a point to check in with Jude before or after a future class to find out whether further intervention is needed.

Once the immediate situation has calmed, reconsider your process for partner and group work. Rather than instructing students to create their own, do this for them. This prevents any student from being left out or feeling anxious about being asked to work with their peer(s). You may choose to assign students at random, you could choose to use groupings based on birth month or favorite ice cream flavor or another arbitrary detail that all students would have an opinion on, or you may wish to partner or group students in ways that seem arbitrary but that encourage teamwork and ensure that students who may learn from another's traits consistently interact with that person.

Next, ascertain whether the comments about Jude's mom were a momentary and passing situation that has been solved by redirecting the students or if this is an ongoing concern. Rather than lecturing the class (likely causing students to blame Jude for this), intentionally incorporate as much diversity into the classroom as possible. This may be focused on LGBT+ status, race, ethnicity, types of abilities, etc. and it may also be focused on all other types of differences and how differences are good for society. For example, if you are dividing younger students into groups based on their favorite ice cream flavor, take a moment to talk with younger students about why it is good for the ice cream business that people like different flavors and how it is easier to share if people do not want the same thing at the same time, since it means no one gives up their favorite. If students are older, encourage them to consider how diverse learners may interpret the assignment differently or how coming from a different culture may lead to different results in a group work setting. Your goal is not to divert from your intended lesson plans, but rather to be intentionally and mindfully encouraging students to think about all of the ways diversity exists around them. This will allow them to begin to view differences, to see how these can lead to benefits, and to be more open to positively considering their own uniqueness as well as that of their classmates.

Scenario 14

After being at your school for a number of years, you have become known for advising several extra-curricular activities and groups. One day during lunch, a handful of students approaches, asking if you would advise a group they want to start. They tell you it requires no effort on your part; the group will meet weekly during lunch in your classroom or office, they just need to write your name down on the application form for group approval and get you to sign it. You check your calendar and tell them that you can host their new group every Thursday. When they hand you the form for your signature, you find out that the group is a Gay–Straight Alliance.

1. If you were the sole decision-maker at your school, how would you choose for your school to handle this situation?

2. Based on what you know of those in decision-making positions at your school, what decision do you think they would make about how you must handle this situation?

3. Utilizing only your school's student handbook and staff handbook, what (if anything) do they dictate about how you must handle this situation?

4. If the answer to question #1 is different from the answers to question #2 and/or question #3, what can you do, in your role in the school? What (if anything) should you do?

SCENARIO 14.1

Would your answers to the questions be different depending on the age or grade of the students? If so, at what ages would the answers change and how? If not, why not?

GUIDANCE

Depending on your school, this may not even require any guidance! In many schools, these organizations have existed for many years without incident or concern. If your school is open to this group—and since you have read this book—you are a great fit for this, and it sounds like your students are excited to lead the creation and ongoing meetings, so just continue to support them the way you do all of the other groups you've advised!

If your school refuses the application to begin the group, work with the school to find out their reasoning. Consider involving community leaders and the student participants' guardians as needed. You can also offer the school information about other schools in the news who refused to allow this type of group and the ways in which it became problematic to refuse to allow all groups to gather if they meet the school's group creation requirements.

Incorporating Scenario 14.1, the age or grade of the students may matter here. High school students may choose to be more vocal about their feelings on the school's initial refusal. They may need to be talked with to ensure that they do not respond to the school in a way that can get them into trouble. Middle school students may want to partner with their guardians for support in fighting against the school's discriminatory policy. At the elementary level, students may not at all understand why they are being rejected by the school, making it even more necessary to create an ongoing dialogue with those raising the students to ensure that accurate information is getting home about what is happening at school.

At any age, talk with students before involving their guardians and incorporate mindfulness when discussing the situation outside of the group wanting to start this gathering. Not every student participant may identify as LGBT+, and it may not be safe for some to be assumed to. In addition, it is never okay for anyone to out another person, so it is crucial to have ongoing conversations with students about how to speak up for what they believe is right without making choices that jeopardize their own or someone else's safety or academic career.

Scenario 15

Each month, your school hosts a guest speaker. You are not sure who chooses the speaker or how the order is set; you simply know that you are tasked with being one of several staff members to sit in the auditorium and keep the students quiet and seated during the presentation. At today's assembly, the guest speaker talks about the importance of family. As the person continues to talk, they begin to discuss the importance of having a mother and a father in the home. They stress that students without both mothers and fathers working together to raise a child, the child will grow up lacking life skills and being a lesser-quality person than their peers. When they give examples, the speaker talks about how girls should be learning to cook and keep the house from their mothers and boys should be growing up learning to mow the lawn and fix the car from their fathers. You know that there are students and staff in the auditorium whose homes include same-sex parents, single parents, and parents who teach non-traditional roles to their children.

1. If you were the sole decision-maker at your school, how would you choose for your school to handle this situation?

2. Based on what you know of those in decision-making positions at your school, what decision do you think they would make about how you must handle this situation?

3. Utilizing only your school's student handbook and staff handbook, what (if anything) do they dictate about how you must handle this situation?

4. If the answer to question #1 is different from the answers to question #2 and/or question #3, what can you do, in your role in the school? What (if anything) should you do?

SCENARIO 15.1

Would your answers to the questions be different depending on the age or grade of the students? If so, at what ages would the answers change and how? If not, why not?

GUIDANCE

This situation may make you feel the need for immediate intervention. Some readers may already be envisioning themselves yelling out from the darkened auditorium, arguing with the speaker, making a rousing speech about inclusion, and the speaker leaving in a disgrace while the students all cheer for inclusion. A great closing scene for a movie, no question, but this is not really realistic. Instead, consider the ramifications of letting the speaker finish and then addressing the situation as a school. Maybe this means a schoolwide announcement that acknowledges that families are absolutely important and that families can look very different to the ones described by the speaker but that they are all equally valuable. Maybe this means you find ways to incorporate the value of different types of families and people into your lesson plans or class discussion for the next several days, to challenge the idea that a family can only look one way. Speak with your supervisor to ascertain whether the school will be addressing this as a whole or whether you will need to speak to colleagues individually to share your concern and ask them to impart more inclusion in their classrooms to undo this narrow-mindedness on a smaller scale. Finally, talk with the school to find out who chooses speakers and how the speakers are vetted before being chosen. Find out about creating a checklist of requirements in order to approve a speaker. You may even ask to be on the committee choosing or verifying speakers in order to ensure this does not happen again.

Scenario 15.1's question about ages or grades of students does not change anything regarding the need to respond and ensure that all students' families are validated. It simply impacts how the message is shared. When talking with students after this type of event or situation, focus on their comprehension level. Having a second grader draw their own family and write what makes their family great would be age-appropriate, having a tenth grader do this would likely seem off the mark to that student. In addition, older students may be more open to discussing different types of families using television or film families rather than sharing the inner workings of their own families with their peers. You can offer assignments or discussion topics based on the ages and sense of privacy that different age ranges tend to prefer. This keeps the conversation going without causing students to feel forced to reveal what they may believe to be family secrets.

Scenario 16

Like many schools, yours now has regular active shooter practice drills. You are new to the school. Your role during these drills is to go to the cafeteria and guide the children to a safe, less open space. This space has been designated to be the nearby locker rooms. As per the instructions, you are supposed to send the male students into the boys' locker room and the female students into the girls' locker room. Today is the first drill of this year, and it is the first time you have been assigned this role. During the drill, as you direct the students, one student points to another and says, "What about Dakota?" You remember that Dakota is transgender. While Dakota identifies as a girl, Dakota's school records have a male designation. In addition to making a decision very quickly for the purpose of this drill, you also want to make the right decision and make a great first impression on your new boss.

1. If you were the sole decision-maker at your school, how would you choose for your school to handle this situation?

2. Based on what you know of those in decision-making positions at your school, what decision do you think they would make about how you must handle this situation?

3. Utilizing only your school's student handbook and staff handbook, what (if anything) do they dictate about how you must handle this situation?

4. If the answer to question #1 is different from the answers to question #2 and/or question #3, what can you do, in your role in the school? What (if anything) should you do?

SCENARIO 16.1

Would your answers to the questions be different depending on the age or grade of the students? If so, at what ages would the answers change and how? If not, why not?

GUIDANCE

In an active shooter drill or a drill related to any safety concern, the sole goal is to keep all students safe. While it is understandable that you want to do a good job for your supervisor, this is not about you. It is about safety. That's it. As such, all that matters is that every student is brought into a locker room during the drill. Since many transgender students experience bullying in school, it is important also to maintain Dakota's safety during the time spent in the locker room. Your goal is to make it safe for every student to go into the locker room that matches their gender identity. This means that Dakota should be instructed to go with the girls into the girls' locker room. If there is not a staff member going to each locker room, but there is the option for you to choose which to go into to sit with students, go into the locker room with the transgender student any time there is a transgender student involved. This helps to ensure their safety during the drill in case there is any cause for concern. As a result, all students will be in the locker room, per your duties to move them into these locations, and Dakota and any other current or future transgender student(s) will be kept safe during the drill itself.

Although Scenario 16.1 asks you to consider age or grade, safety drills are not based on this since the unsafe situation is not likely impacted by a student's age or grade. Your role during safety drills is always to keep the students safe. This occurs in two parts: safety from the current threat causing the drill and safety during the drill. By ensuring that all students go into the area designated as the safest option, you are keeping them safe from the current threat. By reaffirming the transgender student's gender identity by directing them to the locker room that aligns with their identity and by proving adult supervision in that space, you are keeping the student safe during the drill.

Once the drill is over, speak with your instructor about whether there is an existing policy for these situations in regard to transgender students. If not, ask to write it or to be part of the group that writes it. If there is a policy and it is not inclusive, ask to rewrite it or be part of the group that rewrites it. If the policy is inclusive, encourage the supervisor to make sure all staff are aware of the policy so that there is no confusion or mistakes made in the event of a future drill or true emergency. You may even wish to include this information where you keep your student roster and any emergency drill instructions so that you and anyone who may be with you during this time have easy access to this.

Put Your Knowledge into Practice

Section summary

This section takes the foundational knowledge and the scenario hypotheticals and turns them into real-life action within your school(s). While it is understood that the readers of this book work within a wide variety of academic and educational roles, the intentions for this section are to allow you to become more mindful of the realities of your spaces and the information being disseminated to your school's community so that you can make intentional decisions within the scope of your position to best support LGBT+ people.

How to use this section

Some chapters will apply to all, regardless of their role within the school. Others are specific to school subjects or job roles. You are encouraged to focus on the chapters most applicable to your own role, while also being mindful of the recommendations and guidance that benefits your colleagues, superiors, and those whom you supervise. While focusing on one's own scope of work is logical, understanding where there is opportunity for others can allow for an overarching change within schools, and it allows folks to support one another as they advocate for transformations within their own school roles.

Section take-away

This section offers the reader a way to assess their school's current inclusiveness, offers guidance on improving the physical space, policies, and protocols, and provides suggestions on classroom alterations to create a supportive and affirming environment.

8

Assessing Your School

Although the previous sections may already have your mind swimming with ideas for change, before beginning to work to implement these ideas it is vital to become mindful of all of the areas in need of change. Some readers may be reading this book individually, while others may be reading it as a teachers' cohort, an entire school staff, an all-district mandate, or an entire city or state collective. Whatever your individual experience, you may wish to seek out a trusted colleague or suggest working together as a small group to assess your school, both so that there are a variety of opinions weighing in and so that there is already a contingent in place to begin the change process once the needs for change are fully recognized.

It can be easy to want to go back in time as far as possible when considering ways in which your school could improve upon its inclusion practices. However, this can result in significant frustration of wishing things would have been done differently when the focus now should be what can be done differently today and what can be set up so that situations occur differently moving forward. With this in mind, decide to consider the past one or two years and do not become distracted by what has occurred in the school before then, unless there's been a specific incident in your individual school or school district's history. It is likely that your school has not changed its ways significantly in the past one or two years, so this allows for the consideration of continuity rather than focusing on something that may have occurred only once for a specific need for that school year.

First impressions

Although it can be easy to want to jump right into the school itself, begin by considering the experience of students and their families, as well as LGBT+ staff members. Pretend that you are brand new to the district. Obtain documents that would be provided to enroll a new student. Examine those documents carefully with the new inclusive knowledge you have. How many gender-marker boxes are on the form? Is there a place on the form for a child whose name is not the same as the name on their birth certificate? How are the spaces worded for who the parents or guardians of the child are? When legal documents are required of any guardians, is there a space on forms for gender inclusivity and to document the names the individual or individuals use, if these are not the same as on legal documentation? Are there any other areas on any of the forms that would indicate to an LGBT+ family that a person who identifies as such is anything less than fully welcome?

Now, look into the hiring processes of your school or school district. First, begin by researching where a job opening is posted. This may be something you can access directly, or it may require you to reach out to the human resources department. If the information is listed only on the school or department's website, look at the website through the eyes of an LGBT+ person. Is there information on the website that indicates whether the school district is inclusive? Is there wording on the website that only engages people who fall into the gender binary? Are there photos or drawings of educators or school attendees? Do those images depict different types and appearances of people? Now, review the job posting itself and other postings for other jobs. Are you seeing any wording that indicates whether or not the school or role is inclusive? Frequently, non-discrimination policies are listed either at the bottom of individual job posts or somewhere in the job board section of the website. Do you see that? If so, is the language fully inclusive, containing protections for individuals regardless of sexual orientation and gender identity? If the job is posted in places other than on the school's or district's website, where is it posted? If it is posted in public newspapers, websites, or magazines, take time to review those. Who is the audience for each? What are the images of people depicted in each? Does your community or city have a location-specific LGBT+ newspaper, magazine, or website? If so, does the school post job openings there with the same frequency they post them to non-LGBT+ specific places?

Next, examine the job application process itself. Some schools still require handwritten documents. If yours does, request to review one from the human resources department. (They are typically standard for all positions within the school or school district, with additional department-specific paperwork required.) If the job application process is electronic, review this instead. As sexuality is typically not questioned or documented on the majority of job application paperwork, review the documents as if you were a person whose gender identity does not match the information on their legal documentation, such as a birth certificate or Social Security card, documents that are required to prove identity when being hired. On the application paperwork, is there a gender-marker question? If so, how many options are available? Is there a place for an applicant to document that they use a name that is not the same as the name on their legal documents? Is there a place to document that their diploma, teaching license, or work experience was awarded to or occurred under a different name? As you review these, also look to see whether the electronic process, if there is one, allows an applicant to continue to complete the paperwork if they leave a question blank. In some cases, for example, where the available gender options are binary, a person may feel they have no choice but to leave that question blank if neither of the two options are applicable. However, if the computer program does not allow the applicant to continue applying without answering that question, this is important to note.

Next, try to speak with someone in the hiring department to find out whether the school has any record of a transgender person applying. Find out if the hiring department receives any training in the event of such an applicant and how they would handle it if the name on legal documents does not match the name on the application. In schools where staff are assigned an email address that includes the person's name, find out how the human resources department would instruct the technology team to create an email address for a person whose legal name and the name they use do not match. Also, ask what the process is to change that email address in the event of a name change. It is likely that there is a procedure for this, as it is common for some married people to change or add to their last name. However, the information sought after here would be more aligned with the changing of a person's first name, as would occur in the event that a staff member began to use a different name that better aligned with their gender identity during the process of coming out and/or transitioning.

Now, let's consider the experience for someone who has been enrolled in or hired at your school or school district.

First, let's focus on the students and their families. Does your school have any sort of orientation for new students? In some school districts, these occur before the beginning of each school year to allow students and their families to meet their teachers and become acquainted with a school building. In other schools, these only occur for new students. In some others, these occur toward the end of the school year for students who are finishing a grade at one building and entering a new school building the following year. The intentions for these are typically to have the students tour the school and interact with current students who may be members of a volunteer group, the student council, or other peer group. Obtain a copy of the agenda for any of these orientations. If there is paperwork that exists to train the teachers or that the teachers use to train tour participants, examine those as well. Are these documents preparing to welcome all types of families? Do any prior written speeches or scripts include phrases such as "ladies and gentlemen," which would not include people whose gender is non-binary? Are groups ever split based on gender?

Also, examine any flyers or emails that are sent out to alert families to these orientations. Is all language inclusive to allow all family types to know that all guardians and types of parents are welcome? In some schools, the phrase "moms and dads" is used on the invitation. As you can imagine, this can bring stress and anxiety in single-parent households, in homes in which parents are the same gender identity, and in homes where the guardian or guardians are someone other than traditional parental figures. In these cases, it may be as easy as replacing these words with the word "families." This allows anyone who identifies as the student's family to understand that they are welcome to attend. In addition, does your school offer a website or emailed or mailed newsletter to alert families about important school dates and events? Often students and their families access this information before they ever come into contact with anyone from the school or visit the school itself. It is important to review these documents for inclusive wording and policies. Just as with orientation, you will want to consider and look for any wording about families that may not be fully inclusive.

You will also want to look for any information that is gender based. This may be in relation to if or how the students are divided for field trips or group activities, during health class or sexual education training, or in relation to other large group events in which smaller groups may be formed. In many of these, there may be the non-discrimination legally provided. This may vary based on state, school district, or individual school as some of this may be mandated by law in some places and by the school or school district in others. If this policy is listed anywhere, are "sexual orientation" and "gender identity" listed within the non-discrimination policy?

Now, let's consider staff training or orientations. Is there a process for training or introducing new staff? If so, what is this process? Does this have mandated paperwork to complete? In some schools, this is where new staff would complete paperwork regarding health insurance, which may list family members' names. In other cases, staff may complete emergency contact forms. If your school requires either, review those documents. In some cases, health insurance paperwork may be mandated by an insurance company or by the federal government. In these situations, the documents may not be able to be altered to become more inclusive. However, there is nothing to stop a school from including a note in the paperwork packet to acknowledge that these forms are not fully inclusive and to articulate why the school is unable to alter them to make them such. While this does not change the form, it does allow the individual to recognize that the school is aware of the problematic language and that they do not support this wording. On the emergency contact forms, how are the options worded there? Is the assumption that a person would be listing their spouse or their parents? Many LGBT+ people have someone else who knows them best and would best represent their wishes in the event of an emergency. In addition, it is possible that some would prefer to include information regarding anyone they do not wish to have contacted, even if that person may be considered their legal next of kin. Is this an option on the existing paperwork?

During an orientation or introduction-to-colleagues experience for someone new to the staff, what information is pre-prepared? At some schools, a name tag is already typed and waiting for each individual when they arrive. If your school offers this, where does the school get this name information from? While this can be problematic for someone who does not use the name on their legal documents, this not only impacts those whose gender identity does not match; it can also impact people who prefer a shortened version of their first name, who go by their middle name, or who may otherwise want to begin their collegial relationships using the name they identify with.

The written rules

Now that we have new students, families, and staff enrolled or hired, let's take a look at what the school has chosen to put in writing to address behavioral expectations. We will begin with the students, as this is always the focus of schools and educators.

Let's begin with the school's student handbook. These are often sent to new students or all students in advance of the beginning of the school year. Review the non-discrimination policy. Look into the wording of any anti-bullying policies. Are there specific policies related to sexual orientation and gender identity? If there are policies spelled out for bullying based on race, religion, or other groups typically associated with hate crimes, it is important to note whether sexuality and gender are also included. Are restroom policies listed? Is there anything in the policy dictating which students may use which restroom? Is there anything listed about locker room policies? This may apply to anything from gym class to the need to change for a marching band rehearsal or a school play performance.

Next, look at the dress-code section. It is very common for dress-code sections to be divided by gender. Is yours? Is anything in the dress-code policy discriminatory, based on what you have learned about gender identity and gender expression? For example, is hair length mandated for male students? Are there any rules listed about makeup being for female students only or about male students being prohibited from wearing skirts or dresses? Now, take a look at the staff handbook. Look for information about sexual orientation and gender identity protections throughout. You may find this within the non-discrimination policy, in any area that talks about workplace harassment, and/or anywhere that discusses expected dress code. In some public schools, for both students and staff, there may be more protections and fewer dress-code requirements as many schools operate in unison with other schools in neighboring districts or via a statewide policy. In private schools, there may be more room to make individual decisions about discrimination policies, but there may also be more of a need to adjust or adopt dress-code requirements, as many private schools operate independently from all other neighboring schools.

Does your school offer an employee handbook? This may have been handed to staff at the time of their hiring or provided to them during an orientation or training session. Examine this document. Consider the same dress-code areas as may be listed in the student handbook. In addition, seek out information regarding disciplinary policies and expectations. This should be considered carefully, and this part of the staff handbook should mandate how staff members are expected to respond when students break a rule in the student handbook. Is anything listed specifically on how to respond to a student going through a gender transition? Is there anything specific listed on how to respond when a student bullies or harasses a peer or a staff member for their sexual orientation or gender identity? Interactions with student families may also be spelled out in this handbook. Is there anything listed regarding families that are not accepting or affirming of a student's sexual orientation or gender identity? This handbook may also list harassment policies between staff members. What is listed regarding the harassment of an employee based on their sexual orientation or gender identity? If this occurs, what do the handbooks say about how to report the situation and to whom? You may also want to find out if the person meant to receive that report has training that specifically includes sexual orientation and gender identity. Finally, this handbook may offer mandates or recommended guidance regarding how a classroom, classroom/office door, or other student-facing space may be decorated. Are there any rules that would prohibit the inclusion of LGBT+ symbols or the symbols or acknowledgment of support of other minority groups?

Introduction into the learning environment

Now that you've completed a cursory overview of the information that would be provided to new students and their families, as well as the handbook for new staff, you can begin to consider the school experience itself. (If you are an administrator or otherwise work within more than one school building, you will want to do this for each building.) Make this walk through two separate times, once as the student or a student's guardian, and once as a staff member of the school.

Let's begin with the perspective of the student and their family. Does your school offer bussing or other transportation? If so, are seats assigned on the bus and, if they are, how is this done? Are bus drivers trained to interact with LGBT+ students, students who may transition during an academic year (or between academic terms but may ride the same bus before, during, and after transitioning)? Are bus drivers or other transportation professionals trained to speak with families of students who may be non-traditional family types? (Remember intersectionality here and be mindful to examine this for all students, including those who may have different bussing or transportation needs, such as students in wheelchairs and students with developmental delays whose transportation may be differently handled from those of the majority of students. You may also need to assess private transportation companies if your school outsources transportation for some students.)

Once you have considered the experience of how students travel from home to school, it is time to consider the school building. If possible, begin at the front doors of your school or wherever your students enter the building each day, just as a student would and just as their guardian would, when envisioning the experience through their child's eyes. Walk through the halls and keep an eye open for anything that would indicate to them that this school is inclusive and accepting. You may find this in terms of inclusive stickers on front doors, office doors, or classroom doors. You may find this in wording on posters or within the school information prominently displayed in the entryway, or by examining the way the school interacts with the community based on the artwork or informational posters hung throughout the school. Are the families depicted in posters and pamphlets throughout the school inclusive of families that may have same-gender parents or single parents, or families in which the guardians are connected to the children in some other way? If there is information about dating and relationships, do you see same-sex couples? If there are pamphlets about safe sex or domestic partner abuse available, are same-sex couples included? Are the words used within these materials gender-neutral?

Let's consider restrooms. If you were a student at the school whose gender identity does not match the gender they were assigned at birth, would you know which restroom you would be permitted to use? (Would you know this if you were an LGBT+ parent of a student?) If there are multiple restroom options for those with varying gender identities, how far are they located from where a student may be in a classroom? Is it realistic to expect a student to be able to move from the furthest possible classroom to that restroom and back, both without missing significant class time and within the confines of class transition times? Is this significantly different from the experience for students whose gender assigned at birth aligns with their gender identity? Are there spaces in bathrooms and locker rooms for students to have privacy? In classes where students are learning about human development and families, are different types of people depicted in the class material? If so, are they depicted positively and equally to traditional family units?

Let's now consider the experience from the staff perspective, either as an LGBT+ staff member or as a staff member seeking to be inclusive of and affirming to LGBT+ students. Do staff use the same restrooms as students? If not, are staff restrooms gender-neutral? What options do staff have to make changes to their name and gender marker, so it is accurate on forms or other indications of who the staff member is within the school? How is this documented on classroom doors and staff directories, and prepared for the yearbook?

9

In the Classroom and Direct Learning Spaces

Beginning again with the student's perspective, focus now on your space. Based on your role in the school, this location may vary widely from that of your colleagues or professional friends. For administrators, counselors, and coaches, this may be your office. For teachers, this may be your classroom. For those who provide transportation, this may be the same vehicle each day or supplies you bring with you into each vehicle you use to transport students. For other paraprofessionals, those whose work has them moving to the students rather than having a classroom or office of their own, and those in the janitorial or kitchen staff, this space may be a supply cart, a section of the library or computer lab; it may be your cafeteria line or your janitorial closet. For lunch or recess monitors or volunteers, this may be only the clipboard or staff pass you carry with you during your time with students.

As you ascertain what areas or items to focus on for this section of the assessment, think about where you are most often found within the school. Consider where students would find you if they were seeking you out and what you tend to be doing or carrying. The goal here is to become mindful of what message that space or item(s) may represent. Do you have any materials that show support of LGBT+ people? Are there areas where other beliefs or groups of people are shown? (This may be religious, it may be related to the clubs or groups you supervise, it may be in relation to the pioneers of the subject matter you focus on, it may be your personal hero, it may be family photographs at your desk, etc.)

10

Teaching and Learning Materials

In this section, since the focus of education is always on students, it can be assumed that supporting LGBT+ inclusion in the learning space also indicates to students' families and to LGBT+ staff that the learning experience is inclusive of all. As such, there is no need to differentiate here for the perspectives of students, their families, and staff. (Thus, this may be the most cost-effective, efficient, and impactful way to insert LGBT+ inclusion.)

While the legalities of name changes and using the names students request staff to call them varies by city and state, if your school allows you to call "Jaclyn," "Jacky," or "Jay" if they request, it is logical that your school (and/or you) ought to also support students whose requested name is based in their gender identity. On a school attendance sheet or another place where student information is documented for the regular teacher or a substitute teacher, how would a student using a name different from their legal name be listed on the class roster? How is that name changed so that it appears correctly on all student rosters? Not only is this important in general, but this prepares a substitute teacher to correctly call role without accidentally using a student's legal—but not used—name or becoming confused or assuming students are playing a prank if the name this student uses does not appear to match their gender identity based on their gender expression. Is this name used on all student documents within the school's computer system as it pertains to attendance, grading, etc.?

Looking at your specific teaching tools can seem specific to your subject matter or the role you have within the school. If your classroom has mandatory readings (including textbooks, novels, worksheets, etc.), are LGBT+ people mentioned at all? Are there any areas in which LGBT+ people (real or as characters) are utilized? If so, are they depicted positively or negatively? For those whose job focus is administrative, consider your meetings on student learning, student enrichment, curriculum development, and all others that focus on how to better the students' academic experience, as well as those that center on employment, staff retention, and continuing education/training for staff. Are there any that focus specifically on LGBT+ students? Are there any that consider the needs of LGBT+ staff? How many focus on providing guidance for ways to include more LGBT+ awareness or diversity and inclusion? For those whose job focuses on student and staff interaction while providing food, medical, janitorial, after-school, mentoring, or other services, do you receive any training for the specific needs of LGBT+ students or staff?

11

Clubs, Extra-Curriculars, Electives, and Sports

This category can be somewhat tricky. This is because many organizations operate under a state, federal, or international set of rules and standards. As such, it may take significant time to review which opportunities are created and run directly by your school, and thus are available for updated policies, and which are under a larger organization's rules, and which are not. For the purposes of this process, it may be most beneficial to gather or create a list of all activities, divide the list into those that are within your school system's control and those that are not. Then you can assess the way each acknowledges or ignores LGBT+ people. This information may not be readily available and you may be required to reach out to those who run or supervise each group. In order to make the most of your time, this may be a document best compiled by initially reaching out to staff via email to request a document or link to a document that outlines the qualifications, rules, and other specifics of each activity. This will speed up the process of gathering the information, as well as allow you to recognize which activities do not have anything procedural in existence. For organization overviews, you may find this information or the mission statement of the activity listed on the state, federal, or international website representing the vastness of the activity.

In addition, some activities may already be divided into binary gender categories. This is most common in sports. If your school operates under one sports conference, you may not need to seek out information for each individual sport as the conference may have one manual that covers every sport within the conference. If this is the case at your school, you can review that manual, looking for any acknowledgment of LGBT+ people, as well as seeking out information about how a non-binary or transitioning student would be permitted to participate.

12

How to Implement Change

Once you have gathered documentation that recognizes the areas in which your school community is already inclusive, as well as the areas in which there is minor or significant room for improvement, it is time to begin the process of creating and implementing those changes. For some readers, they may be in a position of enough power right this very moment to begin to draft these changes and submit them as new rules. For most readers, however, it may seem you are not in a position of power. As such, it can now feel as if you have become aware of problems but have no opportunity to solve them. Understandably, this can feel very frustrating. However, this does not have to be the case!

Now, you are likely looking at notes from information gathered during the assessment process and notes for how best to reach out to those in power positions to create and implement change. If this feels a bit overwhelming, that is okay! Certainly, if it was your job to make everything happen solely on your own, that would be very big job! However, this is very likely not the case. In fact, there may already be people who support creating a more inclusive and affirming environment. Maybe these are people who have also been required to read this book if that is why you are reading it. Maybe these are people who students have come to know they can trust and count on. Maybe these are other community leaders who frequently donate financially or in kind to various organizations and programs within your school. In addition, you may not know how many students, families, and staff members identify as LGBT+ individuals and/or allies and supporters.

The first step is to take time to recognize who in your school system does have a level of power, either to directly influence or by being in a position to join you in your goal promoting consideration for increased inclusion. This may be an elder who is well respected, it may be someone known for championing new programs within the school, it may be the principal or dean of your school building, it may be the school superintendent, it may be a parent and family group for the school, it may be someone on the school board, or perhaps it is someone beloved by many regardless of their job title. Make a list of anyone who may be influential. Take time to think about the best way to approach each of these people. Some people may warm up best to casual conversation little bits at a time over a long period of time. Others may prefer a more formal sit-down meeting in which information is presented to them. Some may prefer to receive information or requests for support in writing via email. By best understanding how to approach the people you want to buy into making your school more inclusive, you increase your odds of gaining their support.

Since you are reading this book, talking about it can be a great way to initiate these conversations in a casual way. You can begin discussing something you have read each time you bump into a person whose support you are seeking. Maybe you can share a fact, or maybe you prefer to share a thought or opinion you have about some part of the book. This can be a great place for conversation to occur organically, both about the information within this book and as a bridge to have conversations about the thoughts and feelings this book has brought up in you which can be used to ask about a person's thoughts and feelings in response or reaction to yours. For those you think would prefer a more formal approach, either verbally or in writing, the notes you have made while assessing your school can become a great place to begin the conversation. Keep in mind that while you have become significantly more aware of areas of concern in which improvement can occur, you will likely be talking to many whose understanding and awareness of the needs of LGBT+ people may be at or below the level yours was the moment before you began this book. It is vital to be mindful of this so that you offer foundational knowledge to someone unaware without coming across to them as patronizing. If this is not something you feel prepared to provide, you can always refer back to this book for guidance. You can either utilize language from the book as it was provided to you, or you can share the idea that the person you are speaking with may benefit from taking time to read this book by talking about the ways in which you feel you have benefitted from this reading experience.

Here are some sample scripts you can use to reach out to individuals in writing (typically done via email or a school's messaging program) to schedule a meeting to speak with them regarding ideas you have for areas of inclusion improvement:

- I am reaching out to you after having read *The Educator's Guide to LGBT+ Inclusion*. As I read this book, I began to examine the ways in which our school is successfully supporting LGBT+ students, families, and staff. I have also found some ways in which I know we can do better. I would love to schedule a time to talk with you about both. Please let me know when you are available to meet.
- I wanted to reach out to you because I have begun to recognize that our school is not as LGBT+ inclusive and affirming as it could be. I know that, as a school, we pride ourselves in supporting the learning needs of all students, and I would love to discuss ways we can be doing that better. When are you available to discuss this?
- As we gear up to begin another month/semester/year at SCHOOL NAME HERE, I have recognized that we have the opportunity to make some small but impactful changes that would support our school's LGBT+ students, families, and staff. I would very much like to discuss these areas with you and to share ideas I have of how we can make these changes with minimal disruption to existing policies, procedures, and experiences for everyone. When do you have time to talk in the next week?
- I am curious as to whether you have had a chance to read *The Educator's Guide to LGBT+ Inclusion* yet. I just completed it myself, and it highlighted for me where we are doing well affirming and supporting LGBT+ students, families, and staff. I am so proud of us for those! It also helped me to recognize the areas in which we can improve. Let's schedule a time to discuss these!

13

In the Meantime/ On Your Own

While the goal is to be offering information to those in power positions, to be collaborating with colleagues who already support making positive and more inclusive changes, and to be doing the work to get those changes in writing and approved, this can all take time. However, this does not mean you are stuck spinning your wheels! Instead, there are many ways in which you can promote LGBT+ inclusion and affirmation, regardless of your role in the school, regardless of your budget, and without making significant changes to the way you are already doing your job.

Physical space

Whether your space is a classroom, office, cart, supply closet, cafeteria, or other space, small changes may be overlooked by many but will be noticed by those most in need of your support. If you are allowed to use decoration, include images of LGBT+ flags. (Remember that there are a variety of flags indicating support for different people under the LGBT+ umbrella. These include the generalized rainbow flag as well as flags specific to transgender people, agender people, lesbians, bisexuals, pansexuals, and asexuals.) Anywhere your name is listed or written, you can add your pronouns. Typically, they go after your name or under your name and in parentheses. For example:

Harvey Polis (he/him)
Marsha Rivera (she/her)
Gilbert Jones (they/them)

You can place this on your name tag on your staff's mailbox, add it to your name on your door (if you have one), add it to any name tag or identification you wear while in school, and anywhere your name is written. This may be on a handout you provide as an opportunity to get to know your students. The short form may include questions such as:

- How are you listed on my roster? (Your full legal name.)
- What name do you want me to call you?
- What pronouns do you use? (Circle all that apply.)
- Where may I use these pronouns?
  - In class
  - With other school staff
  - In communication with your family
- Would you like to meet with me privately to talk about this?
  - Yes
  - No
- Is there anything else you would like me to know about your name or identity?

For those looking to simply share their own pronouns, they may choose to have them written on the chalkboard or whiteboard on the first day of school, they may be listed as part of a staff or school website where families have access to classroom information, or, if your school lists the cafeteria staff on the lunch menu handout, that is also a place where pronouns can be included. This does not cost any time or money and will likely be ignored by most people. However, those whose pronouns do not match the gender they were assigned at birth or the gender that correlates with their appearance will notice. This is an unspoken acknowledgment that it is safe for them to share their pronouns with you. In other cases, some may notice and inquire. This is an opportunity for you to explain that not everyone's pronouns match the gender they were assigned at birth or their appearance. By explaining this in a matter-of-fact tone, you provide information without judgment and offer them the space to ask additional questions. If you would like to be even more upfront about this, when you begin a school term and are taking attendance for the first time, at the time that you would typically ask students to let you know if you are mispronouncing their name or if they go by something else, you can also ask each student to share their pronouns with you or ask them to go around the room and introduce themselves to you and to the class, where you would find and mark their information on your class roster. This may mean that you first need to explain what you are asking for and why. Since it is likely that your name is written on a board for students to see on their first day, and since you will have already written your own pronouns next to your name, this gives you the opportunity to provide education, and to set the example. You can point to your name to show them what this looks like in writing, and you can begin by introducing yourself using your name and your pronouns. (For example, "I will demonstrate by going first. I am Mr. Brooks, he/him" or "I will demonstrate, I am Mr. Brooks, I use he/him pronouns.")

Inclusive practice in action

One of the quickest ways that a person can make peer interactions more inclusive is to be intentional in the way that groups are created. For decades, it has been common to divide into groups based on gender. Some schools have also offered the alternative option of breaking into groups based on alphabetical order by first name. However, for students whose genders do not match their birth assignment and for those who use a name different to their legal name, this can spotlight these differences. Since grouping is frequently utilized in classroom settings, in gym classes, in staff trainings, and in a variety of areas throughout the educational experience, it is vital that educators have readily available options for creating groups at any time.

Here is a list of useful and inclusive ways to put people into groups:

- *Birthdays:* Divide into groups based on birth month/season, dates of the month, or even day of the week when people were born (thanks to smartphones, this can be an easy question to answer via a search engine).
- *Animals:* Have people group based on favorite animals. This can be random animals (example: dolphins or alpacas or anteaters), or it can be based on animals of the same color (example: turtles or lizards or newts), with you choosing as many animal options as you need to have number of groups.

- *Alphabetically:* Use the last letter of their last name, the name of their favorite celebrity, or the name of the street they live on.
- *Favorite flavor:* You can use this one in a variety of categories: ice cream, candy, juice, soda, salad dressing, etc.
- *Color:* Use shirt or shoe color, backpack color, or other color item that everyone has, allowing for quick division.
- *Magical wishes:* Offer a list of options of what someone would wish for if they had a magic wand. Create groups based on these options. Examples may include the ability to fly, invisibility, zillions of dollars, having a pet unicorn, and others. (You can also allow someone in the room to select a provided number of options for the collective to choose between.)
- *Food:* You can choose a category (for example: vegetables, fruits, desserts) and have them group this way or offer a variety of options within one category to choose, based on their favorite (for example: apples, bananas, grapes, or pears).
- *Would you rather:* Get creative based on your audience or elect someone in the room to come up with ideas! (For example: Would you rather swim in chocolate sauce or cheese sauce? Would you rather sleep in every day for a week, stay up late every day for a week, or not have any homework for an entire week?)

The goal of this is to offer opportunities to group participants quickly and efficiently without highlighting their gender differences or other aspects of their personal identity that they may wish to keep private or in which they may have a different experience from the others in the room. By creating groupings based on personality traits, this not only gives the groups something in common instantly, but it also prevents any individual from feeling left out or from not being picked to join a group or a team.

14

Inclusive Curricula

While many of us wish it was possible to either do away with current textbooks or swap them out for books filled with inclusivity and affirmation, this can be cost-prohibitive. In addition, as many schools must utilize the same educational materials for years or decades, a change to the materials would require significant amounts of work on the part of the educators as lesson plans, slides, and other documents would all need to change in order to support and supplement these materials. This can be unrealistic for many schools, and it can put an undue burden on educators who are already frequently overworked. As such, until the time when your school is considering or planning to replace/update their materials anyway (at which time advocating for inclusive materials is vital), it is important to discern how to take existing lesson plans and texts and make them more inclusive. The goal is inclusivity, but the secondary goals are to make changes that require little to no time, effort, or supplies. This makes the change as seamless as possible without adding stress onto educators.

Math

It can be easy to assume that there is no room for alteration here, as most math categories are very specific in their formulations. Although this is accurate, check areas where word problems are given. Are naming pairs all male/female? If so, change these so that there are a variety of gender pairings. Are the names all tied to a clear binary gender? If so, swap out some names for gender-neutral names (examples: Carter, Jude, Sam, Max, Kelly, Jamie/Jaime, Dakota). You can also swap some of the pronouns so that different problems offer pronouns that include he/him, she/her, and they/them.

Also, be mindful of stereotypes about those who struggle with or excel in math subjects. Not only is this well researched to be factually inaccurate, but it furthers the gender binary. Promote the idea and ideals that people of all genders can be successful in math classes by celebrating math scholars of different genders, races, and backgrounds within your classroom.

Sciences

This category is broad, based on ages, stages, and school locations. However, you can incorporate inclusion by considering what your class textbooks show about sexuality and gender, if anything. In some schools, students are asked to create research projects using science to prove or disprove something. Be sure to require students to gain teacher approval before beginning their project to ensure that the assignment does not become a platform using outdated or biased research to undermine the reality of LGBT+ people's identities. In other classes, science focuses on categorizing plants, animals, and people. This can be an opportunity to ask students for other ideas of categorizing people or why this categorization is ever necessary or useful. Offering them the opportunity to think critically with your guidance can help them to better learn about the benefits and detriments of labeling individuals.

Make time to promote and highlight scientific scholars, leaders, and inventors of all genders, races, and backgrounds. This may occur via lecture, through homework assignments to research scientists assigned to individuals or groups, or it may be through the posters on your classroom wall that depict important scientific figures. Each is an opportunity to promote the understanding that people of all differences and backgrounds have offered vital scientific contributions that students benefit from to this very day.

Social studies

This category often encompasses a variety of topics within one class or a variety of classes within a school, depending on the age of the students.

Most who teach this subject matter feel as if there is never enough time to impart all of the lessons of history, culture, and other knowledge bases before the end of their time with students. It can feel impossible to be asked to add another topic into an already overstuffed course. However, LGBT+ knowledge can often be added to the current instruction.

For example, if you teach your students about the meaning and use of the American flag and/or the Confederate flag, or if you teach students about state flags, also talk about the flags used to represent LGBT+ people (the rainbow flag has undergone a few iterations, and, as mentioned previously, there are specific flags for transgender people, agender people, bisexual people, etc.). If your classroom acknowledges Black History Month, during the discussion and activities about Martin Luther King Jr., introduce Bayard Rustin. During talk of the risks and bravery of Rosa Parks, introduce Marsha P. Johnson. If students are learning about Emmett Till, teach them also about Matthew Shepard. When teaching about the way that different movements have altered American history, add the LGBT+ movement to the list alongside Women's Rights and Civil Rights. If your class already includes discussions about the Holocaust, make time to include the recognition that some of the people who were sought out and imprisoned were LGBT+ people, forced to wear a pink triangle on their uniforms. If you teach on world history or culture, include having students compare or examine the laws and treatment for LGBT+ people in the history and present day of places they are tasked to learn about. If you teach classes that include politics, include space for discussions on gender discrimination and who impacts and decides whether the current federal protections do/should also protect transgender people. Your goal is not to stop your class to focus on LGBT+ people or to choose which current lessons and topics are less important than LGBT+ knowledge, but rather to include LGBT+ people and their history into the conversations of what you are already teaching. This not only prevents you from needing to make significant changes to your lesson plans, but it also cements the knowledge that LGBT+ people have always existed, they have always been part of history, and they have contributed to today's society just as other minority groups have, even though these groups are so often ignored in standard American textbooks.

English courses

This category covers so many topics through a variety of grades! In addition, many states have standardized testing that covers reading knowledge, the ability to write well, and other skills deemed necessary by state or federal agencies. As such, many who teach in this category are already being taught to teach to the test or to limit or eliminate anything not guaranteed to be on such a test. With many educators' jobs and many schools' funding resting on the results of student testing, this is completely understandable! While it would be quite easy to offer curriculum and lesson plans for entire courses on LGBT+ literature, poetry, and writing styles, in a K–12 setting, many schools would deem them wonderful in theory but not something possible in practice. So let's avoid that. Let's instead seek out where LGBT+ information can be added into existing coursework, thus allowing you to make your classroom spaces more inclusive without adding stress or panic into the requirements and mandates that are already putting so much pressure on you and your students.

As you guide your students in writing stories or personal anecdotes, provide them with examples that come from a variety of writers and tell a variety of stories. Ensure that these include people of color, people with disabilities, and people from non-traditional families. By blending all of these into the materials most often offered in standard textbooks, this highlights the normalcy of differences without requiring you to pause the classroom to focus on a "diversity day" assignment. As your students continue to learn about writing and as they work on assignments in preparation for the written testing and to prove their ability to utilize spelling, syntax, punctuation, and other skills, provide them with writing prompts that require them to put themselves in the shoes of others. Offer them the opportunity to write about a family led by adults who are unlike those at home. Give a writing prompt in which they write a story or journal entry as if they were a person with two moms or as if they were being bullied or as if they were trapped in the wrong body. By offering them the chance and space to examine life from someone else's perspective, you can give them the tools to become more empathetic and to become more mindful of the ways in which others live and experience life, both including LGBT+ people and anyone who is different in any way.

Many schools provide educators with mandatory reading lists. If yours only offers books and poems by white authors or men or heterosexual people, consider discussing this with the decision-makers at your school. In the meantime, offer opportunities for students to compare and contrast written work by pairing a common book or book passage with something not required. For example, they could compare a section on the daily life experiences of a young girl from *The Diary of Anne Frank* with the daily life experiences of a young girl in *Being Jazz: My Life as a (Transgender) Teen*. Students can compare the opinions or beliefs of Atticus Finch with today's beliefs about transgender people, allowing them to examine gender roles even further than their textbooks typically require. You can even take this a step further by asking the students to compare the lives of these two with their own life. If students are reading poetry by Emily Dickinson, have them compare one of her pieces with one by Audre Lorde.

The goal is not to deviate from what they are already learning; it's to enrich their learning by connecting it to present and past LGBT+ figures. This way, your lesson plans about character development, motivation, the protagonist and antagonist, and relating the characters' stories to those of the students' own lives never has to change. You are simply adding another layer of comprehension and real-life connection to their learning process!

Foreign languages

Take a look at the way you introduce and guide your students in the areas of the world where the language(s) you teach is spoken. In some American K–12 schools, there is a significant portion of the classroom experience that considers the geographical location, culture, and behaviors of people fluent in a language being taught. These can be great places to add in aspects of the LGBT+ experience in age-appropriate ways. For example, if you are teaching students to compare another culture to their own, you could ask them to consider the differences between laws or how families are portrayed in the media. You could discuss politics or major news in those areas, which may include LGBT+ issues (same-sex marriage is often an easy place to start). For older students, this can be a place to discuss what those countries consider to be human rights, with a focus on the treatment of minority groups (including women, people of color, people with disabilities, LGBT+ people). You can also offer a research assignment in which students are given a political topic or cultural figure to study and present to the class. This can be a place to offer either a list of options that includes LGBT+ people or you can have them research a country and compare and contrast with their own, giving them a list of topics to consider that can include LGBT+ issues.

There is also space to bridge a foreign language with the English language. Not only is this feasible when considering cognates and words English has taken from other nations, but it can also be a space to discuss gendering of words. For example, you could offer discussion space on why English uses a word whereas Spanish has a gendered article and a noun. (Example: "table" and "la mesa.") This can be a place for students to learn about how the Spanish language chose which nouns are given feminine articles and which are given masculine articles. It can become easy to transition from here into ideas and ideals of femininity and masculinity in people and how this can vary from nation to nation. There has long been a question to many Americans as to whether a stylishly dressed man is gay or European. What behaviors and traits in one country may indicate something very different in another? In what ways do people in the countries most fluent in the language you teach present differently from people in America? By giving students space and direction to examine what they know from their lives and how that knowledge may be wrong if they were to move to another country, you are teaching students not only directly about LGBT+ issues and people, but you are also guiding them to reexamine their assumptions of gender norms and gender roles, which supports LGBT+ people in America.

Physical education

So often, this part of school is stressful for students. While there are always a few star athletes, many students of all genders and orientations struggle with the expectations of physical fitness within a peer environment. First, consider whether changing clothing for the class is truly necessary. Some schools now simply require clothes with easy movement and rubber-soled shoes. As such, students have the choice to bring a change of clothes and/or shoes or to dress for the day in preparation for this class. This can lessen anxiety about which locker room to change in and how to obtain and maintain privacy, not only for LGBT+ youth but for all who may not feel comfortable in front of their peers while in various stages of nudity.

Next, consider the way teams are created. Not only can you utilize the list of groupings provided in the In the Meantime/On Your Own section, be mindful that opportunities for students to choose their own teams or groups always lead to some students being picked at the end of the process, causing significant stress and anxiety. By pre-grouping students or by dividing them yourself, students avoid the experience of being placed in a hierarchy of importance or value by their peers. In addition, consider ways to encourage students whose physical fitness may not meet the expectations or requirements set by the school. If these are set elsewhere and are not within your control, plan to discuss this with decision-makers but also work to find ways to support the experiences of students who may not have many successes in a gym class setting. Offer opportunities to be the scorekeeper, to set up the equipment, to be the coach of a group, or to keep statistics. Allow students to let you know if they are interested in this or offer the opportunity privately so that no student feels as if you do not believe they are capable of another role. Then vocally support and encourage students in each role during class, from cheering on a great play on the court or field to thanking the scorekeeper to appreciating the way the team coach boosts their team with positivity. This can show all students the value of everyone's contribution without forcing some students to always fear being the weakest player on every team or being the person whose lack of physical prowess may be attributed to their gender identity or sexual orientation.

Music (including general music, various bands and choirs, school musicals, and others)

This category is intended to recognize the wide variety of music-based courses taught as mandatory, elective, and extra-curricular activities in schools. Many schools utilize the same materials for decades, both because there are so many classical composers and pieces and because many school performances focus on holiday classics and/or school or state fight songs in support of sports teams. While this is understandable, there is often also space for educators to discuss music history, lyricists, and playwrights with students.

This is a time in which music history can consider the experiences of women and people of color during a time when roles were typically filled by white men. It can look into whether lyrics may have been assumed to be rooted in opposite-sex/opposite-gender love but may not actually specifically state this. It is a time to consider musical theater and the variety of shows that include non-traditional relationships. These include *RENT*, *La Cage aux Folles, Fun Home, The Prom,* and many others that have music which may be familiar to your students. You may even find that one or more of these musicals have a song or medley in the school's music library, allowing you the option of including one or more in a school choir performance or to use the song as a stepping stone to request the show for an upcoming school musical.

In addition, utilize current music in a variety of genres. Here, you can discuss either individual songs' lyrics or consider the impact on an entire genre, such as songs by Garth Brooks talking about the freedom to choose whom to love, Macklemore and Ryan Lewis singing about same-sex marriage directly, or when rappers or country music artists come out as bisexual or gay. You can also have students focus on the societal impact that can be had when a popular performer includes same-sex couples in their lyrics or when a popular performer's appearance goes against gender norms. Prince, Gladys Bentley, and David Bowie were great examples of this, as were/are Freddie Mercury, Janelle Monáe, Pete Burns, Annie Lennox, Boy George, Big Freedia, and Grace Jones.

The goal here is not to alter the standards and sounds expected of your students but rather to consider the ways in which you can guide students to understand that sexuality and gender expectations and norms have always existed and they have always been woven into the fabric of music and performance. By tying these ideas from music history into students' current favorite artists and songs, students can better understand the emotions and social statements that were made when past artists were identified as LGBT+ or when they spoke out in support of LGBT+ issues and people.

Opposition

Although this book is intended to be educational, guiding, and inspiring, it would be unwise to pretend there is no chance of opposition in response to the goals and efforts of making spaces and classroom materials more LGBT+ inclusive. By recognizing this as possible, we can better prepare for the situation if and when it occurs. This allows for a calm and intentional response, rather than an off-the-cuff remark or statement made in anger which could become more combative than helpful in moving equality forward within your school.

Let's take a look at the stakeholders and where their opposition may stem from and how to respond to it.

School district leaders (including superintendents and school board members)

Depending on the area, those in powerful positions may have little or no direct involvement with your school's students and staff. They may also spend their time managing political expectations and aspirations, writing policies and procedures, and/or otherwise basing their work on many aspects of education that are not necessarily aligned with the realities of in-school experiences and needs. This is typically not an intentional disconnect, but rather an unfortunate byproduct of overworked individuals trying to juggle a variety of responsibilities and decisions without enough time to regularly engage with those who work in the schools, those whose children attend the schools, or those who attend the schools themselves.

If opposition happens here, begin from a place of offering guidance. Perhaps the concern is that making room for LGBT+ inclusion means undermining the current goings-on of the school. Perhaps the concern is that adding LGBT+ inclusion means lessening the focus on areas where state and federal testing requires high student scores in order to continue to receive funding. Before responding to the complaint, clarify what the person is afraid of. This will allow you to respond to their anxieties. It may be helpful to recommend a copy of this book to offer them the foundational knowledge that may provide them with enough understanding to recognize the importance of LGBT+ inclusion in schools. It may be helpful to offer them the most recent studies on LGBT+ youth bullying and suicidality. It may also be helpful to offer to show them ways in which you are incorporating LGBT+ people and history into your classroom or school building without it costing time or money. This way, either you can end their apprehension or you can know that the stress comes not from a lack of knowledge but from a difference of opinion and priorities.

While there is not always a way to convince top leaders to understand and appreciate the ways in which adding in conversations about diversity and inclusion benefits students and staff, by framing the focus on the benefits of student and staff mental health, by tying it to the most recent studies on bullying and suicidality, and by showing how the addition does not take away from testing topics, you are most likely to at least calm them enough to avoid opposition that attempts to remove LGBT+ inclusion from the school. Over time, as they see that budgets and test scores do not change, they may become less interested in whether or not LGBT+ inclusion occurs. Over more time, as they see that, in addition to no negativity, mental health improves or the suicidality rates in the school do not increase, they may even come on board to support the inclusive changes.

School leaders (including deans, principals, and department heads)

Commonly, people in these roles have to walk a line between supporting their school employees and answering to their supervisors. This can place them in precarious positions, especially when a school is working to make changes that can cause waves to start within both groups of people. Often, if their supervisors are supportive of LGBT+ programming, school leaders will get on board, if only because they do not feel it appropriate to second-guess or argue with their bosses. In some cases, when many school employees are supportive of LGBT+ programming, the leaders can ascertain that this offers enough vocal support of the change that it can lead the district leaders to become more open to ideas or more supportive of them. By understanding which side is struggling with this planned change, a person can better assess the hesitation in the school leader(s) at their own school.

In some cases, school leaders struggle with the responsibility of overseeing the numerous changes within their school building. If this is the case, offer to assist. This may be by looking into more inclusive images for the school's walls and website and more inclusive health and sexuality pamphlets for the clinic or guidance office. This may be rooted in working with colleagues to review and amend lesson plans. This may be in offering ongoing support to the school leader through the change process or through offering ongoing auditing and revision of LGBT+ inclusion at regular intervals throughout one or more school years. Find out where the frustration or dread is coming from and do what you are capable of to tackle tasks or provide support.

School employees (including teachers, substitute teachers, paraprofessionals, and staff)

Often, opposition from school employees occurs when it appears that new programs or policies will result in an increased workload to those who are already overworked. It can be easy for them to envision being forced to rewrite every lesson plan, to redo every classroom, and to change every way in which they have been working for the number of years they have been contributing to the success of students in your school. This opposition happens frequently because increased workload often occurs. As such, it is no wonder that some in your school may have an immediate negative reaction to word that LGBT+ inclusion is beginning! Luckily, though, this can be an easy problem to overcome.

First, recommend this book so that they can utilize the same foundational knowledge that you now have. This can help them to understand why LGBT+ inclusion matters. Next, guide them to see how little has to change from their current practices. For example, asking students their pronouns costs no money and takes only a moment longer during roll call on the first day of school. Offer to take time to walk through some of their lesson plans with them to provide guidance on how to incorporate more LGBT+ figures and topics without making any significant changes to the lesson plans that have worked well for them and that have been well received by their students. You can even refer them to the section in this book that fits their subject area, where they can do a quick read to gather ideas. This can help get them thinking while also reinforcing that no one is expecting them to scrap everything and start over, and that plenty of their lesson plans already have room to mention an LGBT+ person or add an LGBT+ person or historical event to the topic of focus. This ought to lessen the anxieties and stress that many may have felt when they found out there were changes coming to the school, without having recognized the minimal amount of effort it would require of them to make those changes in their work.

The other common reason for opposition from staff is one of an argument that LGBT+ people/behaviors/issues go against their personal beliefs. This may be stated as being religiously based, and it may come from the way they were raised; it may be rooted in their culture. While the goal is never to make a person feel uncomfortable in the workplace, it is vital that schools be mindful of inclusion and equal treatment for all, regardless of the personal beliefs of their staff. It may be helpful for those with these concerns to utilize the internet to search for support or education groups for LGBT+ people who share the same religion, background, or culture. This may help to show them that these traits and an LGBT+ identity can exist concurrently. It may be useful to recommend the staff member learn about the changes being made so that they see that the school is promoting inclusion and acceptance, just the way the school promotes this for people of all religions, backgrounds, and cultures.

If the staff member refuses to comply or if you find they have begun to undermine the school becoming more LGBT+ inclusive, it is important to document the situation and to bring it to the attention of their supervisor. It does not benefit anyone when an employee is working against the collective goal and it can be detrimental to the mental health and to the physical safety of LGBT+ students, families, and staff and thus cannot be tolerated. If the staff member is open to learning, shadowing a senior employee may be beneficial as part of a training or probationary process.

If they are not interested in this or if this is not guiding them to become more on-board with the changes to promote LGBT+ inclusion, they may be a better fit for a role that does not interact with students, families, or staff, or perhaps they would be happier working elsewhere.

Families (including parents, grandparents, and other guardians)

Many families have limited information regarding LGBT+ people. Their knowledge base may come from the myths and stereotypes they have heard in their own upbringing or from whatever media or news they choose to watch. This can result in substantial fears. While it can be easy for folks to assume that the negative response comes from someone who is stupid or horrible, the reality is that most families are simply trying to advocate for the safety and success of their own children. Begin by responding to the opposition by assuming good intentions. Offer information about the reason why you are making the choices that they are fighting against. This may occur by providing statistics of LGBT+ youth suicidality and discussing the school's efforts to combat all suicidality by offering the inclusion of various minority groups and via anti-bullying policies. This may come from providing information that talking about sexuality and gender does not actually make a child become gay or transgender. It may be necessary to confront the idea that a child interacting with an LGBT+ person is not suddenly going to become infected with HIV/AIDS. So often, people's misunderstandings lead them to a place of fear. By calmly providing education in a way that is not demeaning, you may end the opposition simply through offering the science and research both to end the misunderstanding and by showing how many different minority groups are discussed and honored throughout the classroom and school, as well as majority groups.

If this does not work, it is incumbent on the school leader to work with their supervisor to handle the matter just as is done every time a parent/guardian complains about something that will not be changed due to that parent's/guardian's complaint. While so many families want to have control over what and how their student learns, schools frequently have to let folks know that their feedback is heard but not going to change how things are done. Whatever tactics are used in all other situations of such requests or demands, they can work here too.

Students

Often, students who speak openly in opposition are either repeating what they hear at home or via the media or are trying to sound tough in front of their peers. If a student speaks up in defiance of LGBT+ inclusive learning material, the change of someone's pronouns, or in any other way, handle the situation publicly and privately. Publicly, address the student in the moment of their behavior, just as you would for any other insubordination. Depending on what occurs and the commonality of the student's behavior, this may be a verbal reprimand or refocusing, it may be to remove them from the classroom, or it may be to give a punishment. This allows all students to see that you will never tolerate this behavior.

However, as the student may be struggling with their own identity or parroting what they hear elsewhere, it is also important to give the student the opportunity to explain themselves privately. Ask the student to stay after class and then ask them to explain their comment or action. Their response may warrant a referral to the guidance office or a heads-up to the school social worker. They may also simply need guidance that these comments do not impress you or their peers and that the punishments will become increasingly severe if the behavior does not stop. Be mindful, though, that punishments fit the situation and that you do not accidentally make the situation worse or reinforce the behavior by unnecessarily including their parents/guardians (if you think this is where the ignorant beliefs stem from). Rather than threatening a phone call home, for example, assign the student an additional writing assignment tied to what was said or done. Perhaps the student must research an LGBT+ pioneer. Maybe they have to write an essay from the perspective of an LGBT+ person their own age. If they used a slur or stereotype, you could have them research the history of that and disprove it. The goal is to provide education and empathy.

Interview with *Parents of Transgender Children* Leaders

An interview with Kathy Blazer, Jennifer Sutton O'Rourke, and star of TLC network's hit show *I Am Jazz*, Jeanette Jennings, the Senior Administrators of *Parents of Transgender Children*, the world's largest supportive community of its kind.

Please tell us about this group!

Parents of Transgender Children was created in 2010 as a community for the parents and guardians of gender diverse children (of all ages) to share resources, experiences, ask questions, and receive support. We come together to offer support, humor, and a sense of solidarity to one another, as we all have experiences to offer and questions to ask. This allows us to learn from each other and to not feel isolated, no matter where we live or how our child(ren) are treated.

You have never granted an interview before and your group is notoriously secret, why?

Part of the success of our community over the years has been because parents have to seek us out to find us. That very willingness to actively strive to find resources to help the parent best affirm their child is often itself the first step to affirmation. Although our group is publicized as a resource in many various places, the group itself has never lent its voice for interviews due to security and confidentiality concerns.

However, the subject matter of the book and Ms. Shane's stellar reputation as an educator, advocate, and unfailing ally to the trans youth community are but a few of the reasons we are endorsing her book. Her book fills a desperate need for the tools necessary for educators to best affirm our children. Simply put, it was too important not to grant the interview.

What do you wish people knew about transgender and gender-variant people?

The most prevalent myths and misunderstandings are based on lack of knowledge and education of gender. Due to rampant politicizing of transgender- and non-binary-related issues, many have already established beliefs that are based on incorrect information. The most common among those are the belief that gender, biological sex, and sexuality are all one and the same. The concept that being transgender is a choice or a mental illness is also sadly common.

You've seen and participated in perhaps hundreds of thousands of conversations about LGBT+ youth in schools. What commonalities can you share with us that we can learn from?

Most of the struggles families with younger children experience within schools stem from the core issue of ostracizing the child seen as "other." The simple day-to-day tasks of using the restroom, dressing for gym class, participating in sports, or even undergoing the now standard active shooter drills results in the child being separated out and isolated for not fitting neatly into their gender binary. Often times, those most guilty of bullying and demeaning the transgender child are those that should be protecting them, the adults, teachers, and administrators.

Typically, when a child begins transition, the first step that families will take is a meeting with the school counselor to make them aware. This is called a 504 meeting, and it includes teachers, counselors, and sometimes professionals such as doctors, therapists, or trans advocates normally follow. Depending on the success of the 504 meeting, the steps that parents take can vary greatly. A supportive meeting can result in a wonderful sense of acceptance, relief, and support for the family and the child. If the meeting is unsuccessful, then petitions may be made to the school board, the department of education for the city or state, or to legal counsel, not to create problems but to ensure that the child is protected as themselves while they are in school.

In addition, too few schools consider the siblings of gender-diverse students. Unfortunately, they are often themselves the targets of ridicule and bullying. This causes distress in both school and home for the entire family. This can result in situations where one sibling gets into fights while defending their LGBT+ sibling or where multiple siblings become targets for bullying, depending on the personalities and sizes of the youth involved. Recognizing this and having plans and policies in place to stop the bullying for both the LGBT+ person and their sibling offers consistent support to every member of the family.

Based on the myriad of conversations you have had within the group, what can school staff, teachers, and administrators do to support transgender and gender-variant youth?

It's really very simple: firmly established trans-inclusive policies and professional training for the staff on gender and sexuality. These are the top decision factors that let families and LGBT+ youth know that the school is safe. Then, hold your employees and yourselves accountable to follow the policies and to consistently update the procedures to ensure that this is a part of the school spirit and school culture. Be mindful of this and upfront about it when hiring new staff so that this is an ongoing recognition so that students and families who begin at the school never have to worry about whether they will remain welcome within the school community.

If you could impart only one piece of advice to all school employees, what would that be?

Our children are more than just their gender. Be aware when you are making classroom plans and assignments that could out or exclude the child. You often spend more waking hours with our children than we do as parents. Affirming and supporting our children can make or break that child's love of learning, their sense of self, and their belief that they deserve a place in this world and for their voice to be heard.

Afterword
by James Lecesne,
Co-founder of The
Trevor Project

The Trevor Project created and operates the largest national 24/7 suicide prevention and crisis intervention lifeline for LGBT and questioning youth. It offers direct contact opportunities for those in need of a trained affirming guide during the darkest of times. It also provides countless resources for LGBT+ individuals and for those who love them.

The Trevor Project's co-founder is James Lecesne. He has spent the past three years traveling around the country as part of an arts initiative called The Future Perfect Project. Through this work, Lecesne and others visit American high schools, LGBTQ+ youth centers, and queer youth conferences, offering true-storytelling and songwriting workshops.

Below, he shares some of his thoughts, as well as how this book correlates with his experiences with hundreds of thousands of LGBT+ youth.

As the co-founder of The Trevor Project, I've been on the front lines as several generations of young people have come of age. During my work as a Trevor Lifeline Counselor, I spent countless hours listening to young people debate the pros and cons of coming out to an unaccepting parent or reliving the indignity of being bullied or questioning whether they should live or die. I took calls from kids as young as 12 who needed to complain about their peers, parents, grandparents, teachers, and church leaders. I listened as young people repeatedly struggled with the same questions, wondering about who to ask to the prom, whether there was a place for them in this world, and, too often, how to manage a mental health crisis. The experience taught me that even the most desperate young person has a talent for living, and often what they needed was someone willing to be in the puzzle with them until they could access their own inherent resourcefulness and wisdom. I've also made it my business over the past 25 years to spend as much time as possible in high schools, listening to young people, collecting their stories, and being a witness to lives that are in the process of becoming.

Although childhood and adolescence are stressful for everyone, for LGBTQ young people, the experience can be even more dramatic, fraught with risks and filled with opportunities to find themselves on the margins or out of step with what some might call "the normative." They are caught between the urge to be themselves and the need to be accepted by their peers, and this is often a perilous path to travel for so many queer kids.

The good news is that there are plenty of places these days where a young LGBTQ+ and questioning young person can seek help and support. While the services offered by The Trevor Project can be vital for those in crisis, it is vital that schools provide safe places in every community where LGBTQ+ youth always know they can go for support and acceptance, regardless of what is happening politically or in their homes. In my experience, schools that have a GSA (Gay–Straight Alliances or Gender and Sexuality Alliances) and sympathetic teachers and guidance counselors are crucial for the wellbeing of these youth. Their guidance can help parents to come around to the understanding that a single supportive adult in the life of an LGBT young person can reduce the chance of that child attempting suicide by nine times.

But the world of LGBTQ+ youth is in a constant state of flux, and even those of us who are working on the front lines are challenged as we adapt to an ever-changing landscape that includes language and practices. Young people are, by their very nature, busy creating the world anew. It is educators' jobs—and the job of all adults—to support this process.

In my experience, most teachers and administrators are doing their best to educate themselves and keep up with these changes, but they are often uncertain about how to support their LGBTQ+ students within the current guidelines provided by their schools and districts. As the guidelines pertaining to LGBTQ+ students vary from school to school and because the laws are always changing on both the local and federal level, a teacher who is not accepting of LGBTQ+ issues tends to rely on their own personal opinion when dealing with an LGBTQ+ student. This not only puts everyone at a disadvantage, it can also lead to that student being shamed, outed, and/or disregarded, thus placing them in grave danger.

The Educator's Guide to LGBT+ Inclusion is a much-needed manual for anyone who has anything to do with LGBTQ+ youth. Kryss Shane has brilliantly illuminated the queer youth landscape and given us a helpful tool with which to navigate this ever-shifting terrain in which most of us are merely visitors.

After reading this book cover to cover, I can honestly say that it ought to be required reading for anyone who wants to participate in the making of that better world. However, this book is not simply a guide for those of us who are already acting as allies and advocates of LGBTQ+ youth; it can be helpful to anyone who has not fully embraced the reality of queer people or for anyone who is struggling with the idea that young people know themselves.

Shane's goal is not to get anyone to change or to provide special treatment for LGBTQ+ youth, but rather to allow queer students the same opportunities that their cisgender and/or heterosexual peers have and to help adults create an environment in which everyone is free to learn, develop, and express themselves within the community. One thing that has become abundantly clear in recent years is that in situations where LGBTQ+ youth feel safe and seen, other students also feel the same and everyone benefits.

Shane provides us not only with the guidance and the ground rules for creating that safe environment, but also detailed examples of the many confounding situations that teachers and educators often find themselves in. With helpful solutions and suggestions designed to minimize conflict and maximize learning, this book can help to create a better world not only for educators but for the students they serve as well.

It is vital to remember that we can and should live out our convictions in positive ways—regardless of who approves. Within our history there are innumerable examples of those who seek tolerance and equality being scorned, laughed at, facing criminal offense and even violence— but history also shows how through courage and determination, love perseveres. This piece of art is meant as an encouragement for those of us who felt defeated to remember that even when it seems that those in power appear to be opposed to equality, we must press on in pursuit of it—and we can do that in many practical ways—in how we live, how we love, and who we support.

Morley, Los Angeles, 2019

Suggested Readings

(Thank you to the New York Public Library, Loyola University Chicago, the Library of the School of Education at University of Wisconsin–Madison, and the Rainbow Book List for their contributions to this compilation.)

Archives and collections

James C. Hormel Gay and Lesbian Center

https://sfpl.org/locations/main-library/lgbtqia-center

This research center is focused on documenting gay and lesbian history and culture through preservation of original materials and by making them accessible to all. The center is a part of the San Francisco Public Library.

Lesbian Herstory Archives

http://www.lesbianherstoryarchives.org

Located in New York City, US, and founded in 1973, this is the oldest and largest collection of lesbian archives.

Arts, literature, and culture

gltbq: An Encyclopedia of Gay, Lesbian. Bisexual, Transgender, and Queer Culture

www.glbtq.com

This searchable encyclopedia includes content, bibliographies, and additional resource links for all things GLBTQ.

Lambada Literary Foundation

www.lambdalit.org

This organization supports and disseminates works written by and for LGBT+ people.

PopcornQ Movies

www.planetout.com/pno/popcornq

This site offers a searchable list of queer films.

Queer Arts Resource

www.queer-arts.org

QAR is a non-profit organization that offers views and discussions of queer art and culture for public education purposes.

Russian Gay Culture

http://community.middlebury.edu/~moss/RGC.html

This site offers literature, films, and history all tied to LGBT people in Russia.

Women in the Shadows: Lesbian Pulp Fiction Collection

http://scriptorium.lib.duke.edu/women/pulp.html

1950s–1960s lesbian pulp fiction is found on this site, powered by Duke University's Sallie Bingham Center for Women's History.

E-journals and online newspapers

Advocate

www.advocate.com

Perhaps the best known and most award-winning LGBT+ website and magazine.

Blithe House Quarterly

www.blithe.com

A collection of gay short fiction is easy to browse on this site.

GLQ: Journal of Lesbian and Gay Studies

http://muse.jhu.edu/journals/glq/index.html

This peer reviewed journal focuses on the LGBT+ perspective.

National Journal of Sexual Orientation Law

www.ibiblio.org/gaylaw

LGBT legal issues from 1998–present.

Gender identity and sexual orientation

Sexual Orientation: Science, Education, and Policy

http://psychology.ucdavis.edu/rainbow/index.html

Here, readers can learn about Dr Gregory Herek's work on homophobia/sexual prejudice, hate crimes, and HIV/AIDS stigmatization. It is also available in French.

General resources

Lesbian.com

http://lesbian.com

This over 20-year-old international website provides links to information on a variety of lesbian-focused information.

Library Q: The Library Worker's Guide to Lesbian, Gay, Bisexual, and Transgendered Resources

https://library.auraria.edu/databases/lgbt-life-full-text

This site is a librarian's guide for working with LGBT+ people. It offers guidance and resources developed by and for library professionals.

Parents, Families and Friends of Lesbians and Gays

www.pflag.org

Also known as PFLAG, this site is the home base of one of the US's most famous advocacy and support groups.

Queer Resources Directory

www.qrd.org/qrd

This site offers more than 25,000 resources about everything queer and is arranged by subject matter.

QueerTheory.com

www.queertheory.com

This site focuses on visual and textual resources regarding a variety of queer and gender studies and culture.

radfae.org: A Web Site for Radical Faerie Information

www.radfae.org

Pulling together Radical Faerie information, this source is geared toward a focus on the spirituality of gay men and their shared beliefs in feminism, prioritizing nature, and how individuals can impact the world.

Stonewall and Beyond

www.columbia.edu/cu/lweb/eresources/exhibitions/sw25

This is an online permanent edition of a Columbia University Libraries exhibit that was created in 1994, in celebration of the 25th anniversary of the Stonewall Riots.

Stonewall Center at UMass Amherst

www.umass.edu/stonewall

This over 35-year-old resource center offers video, audio, and textual information and source materials to combat harassment and discrimination of the LGBT+ community.

TransBiblio: A Bibliography of Print, AV, and Online Resources Pertaining to Transgendered Persons and Transgender Issues

www.library.illinois.edu/staff/collections-information/about/statements/descriptions/lgbt_desc

This transgender-focused site provides resources for and about trans identified people and issues.

History

gayhistory.com

www.gayhistory.com

This website offers an introduction to gay history from 1700–1973. It is an ongoing project that consistently adds new materials.

GLBT Historical Society

www.glbthistory.org

This organization collects, preserves, and provides public access to the history of LGBT+ people as individuals and as a community.

Homosexuality in Early Modern Europe

www.uwm.edu/People/jmerrick/hbib.htm

This is a bibliography on homosexuality in Early Modern Europe, which is organized both by country and by subject matter.

Isle of Lesbos

www.sappho.com/about.html

This is a women-oriented gathering of historical documentation of the lives and views of women both in general and romantically.

Nazi Persecution of Homosexuals, 1933–1945

www.lgbtbarny.org

From the United States Holocaust Memorial Museum, this online exhibit focuses on the experiences of gay people during World War II.

People With a History

www.fordham.edu/halsall/pwh

Offering historical documentation of LGBT+ people, this site offers an international look at LGBT+ history throughout the world and throughout time.

Law

Lambda Legal Defense and Education Fund

www.lambdalegal.org

This American organization specializes in celebrating and honoring LGBT+ people and people with HIV/AIDS through education, litigation, and public policy work.

Lesbian/Gay Law Notes

www.lgbtbarny.org

This journal provides information about ongoing court cases, legislations, and rulings related to LGBT+ people.

Organizations

ACT UP

www.actupny.org

This non-partisan organization aims to end HIV/AIDS stigma and to end the HIV/AIDS crisis.

Bisexual Resource Center

www.biresource.org

This is a resource focused on the bisexual experience and the history of bisexuality via essays and books, plus audio, and visual recordings.

Frameline

www.frameline.org

This organization promotes LGBT+ visibility in the media arts field and hosts the oldest and largest media arts event, called the San Francisco International LGBT Film Festival.

Gay and Lesbian Alliance Against Defamation

www.glaad.org

Now called GLAAD, this is one of the most well-known organizations intended to promote LGBT+ inclusive representation in the media as a way to combat stereotypes and bigotry.

Gay and Lesbian National Hotline

www.glnh.org

This non-profit offers free anonymous information, referrals, and peer-to-peer counselling.

Gay, Lesbian and Straight Education Network

    www.glsen.org

    GLSEN is a leader in the fight against LGBT+ bias in K–12 schools.

Human Rights Campaign

    www.hrc.org

    HRC represents 500,000+ LGBT+ members to fight for their equality.

National Gay and Lesbian Task Force

    www.ngltf.org

    This politically progressive organization works for LGBT+ civil rights.

Religion

Affirmation: Gay and Lesbian Mormons

    www.affirmation.org

    This group has chapters around the world to support LGBT+ LDS members and their loved ones by way of socialization and education.

Dignity/USA

    http://dignityusa.org

    This is the largest and most progressive organization for LGBT+ Catholics.

SUGGESTED READING FOR STUDENTS

The following list includes age recommendations, but remember to consider the reading levels and abilities of your students rather than to rely on age recommendations when choosing which to recommend or include in your classroom. Please note that books should be reviewed by an adult for any potential triggers before being recommended or assigned to students.

General books about LGBT+ issues: non-fiction

Alsenas, Linas. *Gay America: Struggle for Equality*. Amulet, 2008. 160 pages. Ages 12 and older

Bausum, Ann. *Stonewall: Breaking Out in the Fight for Gay Rights*. Viking, 2015. 120 pages. Ages 13 and older

Krakow, Kari. Illustrated by David Gardner. *The Harvey Milk Story*. Two Lives Publishing, 2002. 32 pages. Ages 6–10

Levithan, David and Merrill, Billy, editors. *Full Spectrum: A New Generation of Writing About Gay, Lesbian, Bisexual, Transgender, Questioning, and Other Identities.* Alfred A. Knopf, 2006. 272 pages. Ages 13 and older

Marcus, Eric. *What If Someone I Know Is Gay? Answers to Questions About What It Means to be Gay or Lesbian.* Simon Pulse, 2007. 183 pages. Ages 12 and older

Winick, Judd. *Pedro and Me: Friendship. Loss, and What I Learned.* Henry Holt, 2000. 187 pages. Ages 12–18

General books about LGBT+ issues: fiction

Brothers, Meagan. *Debbie Harry Sings in French.* Henry Holt, 2008. 240 pages. Ages 13 and older

Trueman, Terry. *7 Days at the Hot Corner.* HarperCollins, 2007. 150 pages. Ages 12 and older

Families with gay and lesbian parents or other adult relatives: non-fiction

Combs, Bobbie. Illustrated by Danamarie Hosler. *1, 2, 3: A Family Counting Book.* Two Lives, 2001. 29 pages. Ages 2–5

Combs, Bobbie. Illustrated by Desiree Keane and Brian Rappa. *ABC: A Family Alphabet Book.* Two Lives, 2001. 32 pages. Ages 2–5

Jenness, Aylette. *Families: A Celebration of Diversity, Commitment, and Love.* Houghton Mifflin, 1990. 48 pages. Ages 5–12

Kuklin, Susan. *Families.* Hyperion, 2005. 36 pages. Ages 7–11

Families with gay and lesbian parents or other adult relatives: picture books

Brannen, Sarah S. *Uncle Bobby's Wedding.* Putnam, 2008. 32 pages. Ages 5–8

Caines, Jeannette. Illustrated by Pat Cummings. *Just Us Women.* Harper, 1982. 32 pages. Ages 4–6

De Veaux, Alexiz. Illustrated by Cheryl Hanna. *An Enchanted Hair Tale.* Harper & Row, 1987. 40 pages. Ages 5–10

DeHaan, Linda. Illustrated by Stern Nijland. *King & King.* Tricycle Press, 2002. 32 pages. Ages 5–7

DeHaan, Linda. Illustrated by Stern Nijland. *King & King & Family.* Tricycle Press, 2004. 32 pages. Ages 5–8

Fogliano, Julie. Illustrated by Chris Raschka. *Old Dog Baby Baby.* Roaring Brook Press, 2016. 32 pages. Ages 2–4

Garden, Nancy. Illustrated by Sharon Wooding. *Molly's Family.* Farrar Straus Giroux, 2004. 32 pages. Ages 5–8

Lambert, Megan Dowd. Illustrated by Nicole Tadgell. *Real Sisters Pretend*. Tilbury House, 2016. 32 pages. Ages 4–7

Levine, Arthur A. Illustrated by Julian Hector. *Monday Is One Day*. Scholastic Press, 2011. 28 pages. Ages 2–4

Lindenbaum, Pija. *Mini Mia and Her Darling Uncle*. Translated by Elisabeth Kallick Dyssegaard. R&S Books, 2007. 40 pages. Ages 3–6

Newman, Lesléa. Illustrated by Carol Thompson. *Daddy, Papa, and Me*. Tricycle Press, 2009. 16 pages. Ages birth–3

Newman, Lesléa. Illustrated by Carol Thompson. *Mommy, Mama, and Me*. Tricycle Press, 2009. 16 pages. Ages birth–3

Newman, Lesléa. Illustrated by Laura Cornell. *Heather Has Two Mommies* (new edition). Candlewick Press, 2015. 32 pages. Ages 3–6

Oelschlager, Vanita. Illustrated by Kristin Blackwood and Mike Blanc. *A Tale of Two Daddies*. VanitaBooks, 2010. 40 pages. Ages 3–8

Polacco, Patricia. *In Our Mothers' House*. Philomel, 2009. 48 pages. Ages 6–10

Richardson, Justin and Peter Parnell. Illustrated by Henry Cole. *And Tango Makes Three*. Simon & Schuster, 2005. 32 pages. Ages 3–6

Sima, Jessie. *Harriet Gets Carried Away*. Simon & Schuster, 2018. 42 pages. Ages 3–6

Warhola, James. *Uncle Andy's: A Faabbbulous Visit with Andy Warhol*. Putnam, 2003. 32 pages. Ages 6–10

Williams, Vera B. *Three Days on a River in a Red Canoe*. Greenwillow, 1981. 32 pages. Ages 4–9

Williams, Vera B. Illustrated by Vera B. Williams and Chris Raschka. *Home at Last*. HarperCollins, 2016. Ages 6–10

Families with gay and lesbian parents or other adult relatives: fiction

Freymann-Weyr, Garret. *My Heartbeat*. Houghton Mifflin, 2002. 154 pages. Ages 13 and older

Ignatow, Amy. *The Popularity Papers: Research for the Social Improvement and General Betterment of Lydia Goldblatt & Julie Graham-Chang*. Abrams, 2010. 204 pages. Ages 8–11

Levy, Dana Alison. *The Misadventures of the Family Fletcher*. Delacorte, 2014. 260 pages. Ages 7–10

Levy, Dana Alison. *The Family Fletcher Takes Rock Island*. Delacorte Press, 2016. 259 pages. Ages 7–10

Peters, Julie Anne. *Between Mom and Jo*. Little, Brown, 2006. 232 pages. Ages 13 and older

Woodson, Jacqueline. *After Tupac and D Foster*. Putnam, 2008. 153 pages. Ages 10–14

Woodson, Jacqueline. *From the Notebooks of Melanin Sun*. Blue Sky/Scholastic, 1995. 141 pages. Ages 11–15

LGBT+ children and teens: non-fiction

Andrews, Arin and Lyon, Joshua. *Some Assembly Required: The Not-So-Secret Life of a Transgender Teen*. Simon & Schuster, 2014. 248 pages. Ages 12 and older

Jennings, Jazz. *Being Jazz: My Life as a (Transgender) Teen*. Ember, 2017. 272 pages. Ages 12 and older

Kuklin, Susan. *Beyond Magenta: Transgender Teens Speak Out*. Candlewick Press, 2014. 182 pages. Age 12 and older

Thrash, Maggie. *Honor Girl*. Candlewick Press, 2015. 267 pages. Ages 13 and older

Walden, Tillie. *Spinning*. First Second, 2017. 395 pages. Age 13 and older

LGBT+ children and teens: fiction

Bantle, Lee. *David Inside Out*. Christy Ottaviano Books/Henry Holt, 2009. 184 pages. Ages 15 and older

Beam, Cris. *I Am J*. Little, Brown, 2011. 326 pages. Ages 13 and older

Block, Francesca Lia. *Weetzie Bat*. Charlotte Zolotow Book/Harper & Row, 1989. 88 pages. Ages 13 and older

Bray, Libba. *Beauty Queens*. Scholastic Press, 2011. 396 pages. Ages 13 and older

Brooks, Kevin. *Black Rabbit Summer*. The Chicken House/Scholastic, 2008. 488 pages. Ages 13 and older

Buckell, Tobias S. and Monti, Joe, editors. *Diverse Energies*. Tu Books, 2012. 314 pages. Ages 12 and older

Cameron, Peter. *Someday This Pain Will Be Useful to You*. Frances Foster Books/Farrar, Straus and Giroux, 2007. 229 pages. Ages 14 and older

Cart, Michael. *How Beautiful the Ordinary*. HarperTeen, 2009. 350 pages. Ages 15 and older

Carter, Timothy. *Evil?* Flux, 2009. 264 pages. Ages 14 and older

Cohn, Rachel and Levithan, David. *Naomi and Ely's No-Kiss List*. Alfred A. Knopf, 2007. 230 pages. Ages 14 and older

Danforth, Emily M. *The Miseducation of Cameron Post*. Balzer + Bray/HarperCollins, 2012. 470 pages. Ages 14 and older

Dee, Barbara. *Star-Crossed*. Aladdin, 2017. 277 pages. Ages 9–12

Dole, Mayra Lazara. *Down to the Bone*. HarperTeen, 2008. 367 pages. Ages 14 and older

Downham, Jenny. *Unbecoming*. David Fickling Books/Scholastic, 2016. 375 pages. Ages 14 and older

Farizan, Sara. *Tell Me Again How a Crush Should Feel*. Algonquin, 2014. 296 pages. Ages 13 and older

Farizan, Sara. *If You Could Be Mine*. Algonquin, 2013. 248 pages. Ages 13 and older

Federle, Tim. *Five, Six, Seven, Nate!* Simon & Schuster, 2014. 293 pages. Ages 8–11

Felin, M. Sindy. *Touching Snow*. Atheneum, 2007. 234 pages. Ages 13 and older

Garden, Nancy. *Annie on My Mind*. Farrar, Straus, Giroux, 1981. 234 pages. Ages 12–15

Garden, Nancy. *Hear Us Out! Lesbian and Gay Stories of Struggle, Progress and Hope, 1950 to the Present*. Farrar, Straus and Giroux, 2007. 227 pages. Ages 12 and older

Garvin, Jeff. *Symptoms of Being Human*. Balzer + Bray/HarperCollins, 2016. 335 pages. Ages 14 and older

George, Madeleine. *The Difference Between You and Me*. Viking, 2012. 256 pages. Ages 12 and older

Girard, M-E. *Girl Mans Up*. HarperTeen, 2016. 373 pages. Ages 14 and older

Goldman, Steven. *Two Parties, One Tux, and a Very Short Film about* The Grapes of Wrath. Bloomsbury, 2008. 307 pages. Ages 14 and older

Goode, Laura. *Sister Mischief*. Candlewick Press, 2011. 367 pages. Ages 14 and older

Green, John and Levithan, David. *Will Grayson, Will Grayson*. Penguin, 2010. 304 pages. Ages 14 and older

Griffin, Molly Beth. *Silhouette of a Sparrow*. Milkweed Editions, 2012. 189 pages. Ages 13 and older

Hartinger, Brent. *Geography Club*. HarperCollins, 2003. 226 pages. Ages 13 and older

Hartinger, Brent. *The Order of the Poison Oak*. HarperTempest/HarperCollins, 2005. 211 pages. Ages 12–18

Hartinger, Brent. *Split Screen*. HarperTempest/HarperCollins, 2007. 288 pages. Ages 12–16

Hegamin, Tonya Cheri. *M+O 4evr*. Houghton Mifflin, 2008. 165 pages. Age 14 and older

Howe, James . *Totally Joe*. Ginee Seo Books/Atheneum, 2005. 189 pages. Ages 10–14

Hurwin, Davida Wills. *Freaks and Revelations*. Little, Brown, 2009. 234 pages. Ages 14 and older

Hutchinson, Shaun David. *We Are the Ants*. Simon Pulse, 2016. 451 pages. Ages 14 and older

King, A. S. *Ask the Passengers*. Little, Brown, 2012. 292 pages. Ages 13 and older

Kluger, Steve. *My Most Excellent Year: A Novel of Love, Mary Poppins, and Fenway Park*. Dial, 2008. 416 pages. Ages 12 and older

Knowles, Jo. *See You at Harry's*. Candlewick Press, 2012. 310 pages. Ages 11–14

Kokie, E. M. *Personal Effects*. Candlewick Press, 2012. 341 pages. Ages 14 and older

Kokie, E. M. *Radical*. Candlewick Press, 2016. 437 pages. Ages 14 and older

Konigsberg, Bill. *The Porcupine of Truth*. Arthur A. Levine Books, 2015. 325 pages. Ages 14 and older

Konigsberg, Bill. *Openly Straight*. Arthur A. Levine Books, 2013. 320 pages. Ages 14 and older

Konigsberg, Bill. *Out of the Pocket*. Dutton, 2008. 264 pages. Ages 13 and older

LaRochelle, David. *Absolutely, Positively, Not...* Arthur A. Levine Books, 2005. 224 pages. Ages 12 and older

Levithan, David. *Boy Meets Boy*. Alfred A. Knopf, 2003. 185 pages. Ages 12–15

Levithan, David. *How They Met and Other Stories*. Knopf, 2008. 244 pages. Ages 13 and older

Lo, Malindo. *Ash*. Little, Brown, 2009. 264 pages. Ages 13 and older

Magoon, Kekla. *37 Things I Love (in No Particular Order)*. Henry Holt, 2012. 224 pages. Ages 12 and older

Malloy, Brian. *Twelve Long Months*. Scholastic, 2007. 320 pages. Ages 14–18

McLemore, Anna-Marie. *When the Moon Was Ours*. Thomas Dunne Books/ St. Martin's Griffin, 2016. 273 pages. Ages 14 and older

McLemore, Anna-Marie. *Wild Beauty*. Feiwel and Friends, 2017. 339 pages. Ages 14 and older

Medina, Nico. *The Straight Road to Kylie*. Simon Pulse, 2007. 320 pages. Ages 14–18

Ness, Patrick. *Release*. HarperTeen, 2017. 277 pages. Ages 15 and older

Newman, Lesléa. *October Mourning: A Song for Matthew Shepard*. Candlewick Press, 2012. 128 pages. Ages 13 and older

Peck, Dale. *Sprout*. Bloomsbury, 2009. 277 pages. Ages 13 and older

Peters, Julie Ann. *Far From Xanadu*. Megan Tingley Books/Little, Brown, 2005. 282 pages. Ages 13–17

Peters, Julie Anne. *grl2grl: Short Fictions*. Megan Tingley Books/Little, Brown, 2007. 151 pages. Ages 14 and older

Peters, Julie Anne. *Keeping You a Secret*. Megan Tingley Books/Little, Brown, 2003. 250 pages. Ages 14–16

Peters, Julie Anne. *Luna*. Megan Tingley Books/Little, Brown, 2004. 247 pages. Ages 14–17

Podos, Rebecca. *Like Water*. Balzer + Bray/HarperCollins, 2017. 320 pages. Ages 13 and older

Polonsky, Ami. *Gracefully Grayson*. Disney Hyperion, 2014. 243 pages. Ages 10–13

Rowell, Rainbow. *Carry On*. St. Martin's Griffin, 2015. 528 pages. Ages 12 and older

Ruditis, Paul. *The Four Dorothys*. Simon Pulse, 2007. 243 pages. Ages 12–16

Ryan, P. E. *Saints of Augustine*. HarperTeen, 2007. 308 pages. Ages 14 and older

Sáenz, Benjamin Alire. *The Inexplicable Logic of My Life*. Clarion/Houghton Mifflin Harcourt, 2017. 464 pages. Ages 13 and older

Sáenz, Benjamin Alire. *Aristotle and Dante Discover the Secrets of the Universe*. Simon & Schuster, 2012. 359 pages pages. Ages 14 and older

Sanchez, Alex. *So Hard To Say*. Simon & Schuster, 2004. 230 pages. Ages 12–15

Schmatz, Pat. *Lizard Radio*. Candlewick Press, 2015. 280 pages. Ages 13 and older

Silvera, Adam. *More Happy Than Not*. Soho Teen/Soho Press, 2015. 295 pages. Ages 14 and older

Smith, Andrew. *Grasshopper Jungle*. Dutton, 2014. 388 pages. Ages 14 and older

St. James, James. *Freak Show*. Dutton, 2007. 298 pages. Ages 13 and older

Tamaki, Mariko. Illustrated by Jillian Tamaki. *Skim*. Groundwood Books/House of Anansi Press, 2008. 141 pages. Ages 14 and older

Trueman, Terry. *7 Days at the Hot Corner*. HarperTempest/HarperCollins, 2007. 150 pages. Ages 12 and older

van Dijk, Lutz. *Damned Strong Love: The True Story of Willi G. and Stefan K.: A Novel*. Translated by Elizabeth D. Crawford. Henry Holt, 1995. 138 pages. Ages 14–18

Whaley, John Corey. *Highly Illogical Behavior*. Dial, 2016. 249 pages. Ages 14 and older

Wilson, Martin. *What They Always Tell Us*. Delacorte Press, 2008. 293 pages. Ages 14 and older

Wittlinger, Ellen. *Love & Lies: Marisol's Story*. Simon & Schuster, 2008. 256 pages.
Ages 14 and older
Wittlinger, Ellen. *Parrotfish*. Simon & Schuster, 2007. 294 pages. Ages 14 and older
Wolff, Virginia Euwer. *True Believer*. Atheneum, 2001. 264 pages. Ages 13–16
Wyeth, Sharon Dennis. *Orphea Proud*. Delacorte Press, 2004. 208 pages. Ages 14–17

Sex and gender identity/gender nonconformity

Baldacchino, Christine. Illustrated by Isabelle Malenfant. *Morris Micklewhite and the Tangerine Dress*. A Groundwood Book/House of Anansi Press, 2014. 32 pages. Ages 3–8
Cassidy, Sara. *A Boy Named Queen*. Groundwood, 2016. 77 pages. Ages 7–10
DePaola, Tomie. *Oliver Button Is A Sissy*. Harcourt, 1979. 48 pages. Ages 5–7
DiPucchio, Kelly. Illustrated by Christian Robinson. *Gaston*. Atheneum, 2014. 32 pages. Ages 4–8
Fierstein, Harvey. Illustrated by Henry Cole. *The Sissy Duckling*. Simon & Schuster, 2002. 40 pages. Ages 5–7
Gino, Alex. *George*. Scholastic Press, 2015. 240 pages. Ages 8–11
Harris, Robie. Illustrated by Michael Emberly. *It's So Amazing! A Book About Eggs, Sperm, Birth, Babies, and Families*. Candlewick, 1999. 81 pages. Ages 7–10
Harris, Robie. Illustrated by Michael Emberley. *It's Perfectly Normal: Changing Bodies, Growing Up, Sex & Sexual Health*. Candlewick, 1994. 89 pages. Ages 9–12
Hashimi, Nadia. *One Half from the East*. HarperCollins, 2016. 272 pages. Ages 9–13
Herthel, Jessica and Jennings, Jazz. Illustrated by Shelagh McNicholas. *I Am Jazz*. Dial, 2014. 24 pages. Ages 3–9
Hoffman, Sarah and Hoffman, Ian. Illustrated by Chris Case. *Jacob's New Dress*. Albert Whitman, 2014. 32 pages. Ages 3–8
Huser, Glen. *Stitches*. Groundwood/Douglas & McIntyre, 2003. 198 pages. Ages 12–15
Kilodavis, Cheryl. Illustrated by Suzanne DeSimone. *My Princess Boy*. Simon & Schuster, 2011. 36 pages. Ages 3–7
Mike, Nadia. Illustrated by Charlene Chua. *Leah's Mustache Party*. Inhabit Media, 2016. 26 pages. Ages 3–7
Silverberg, Cory. Illustrated by Fiona Smyth. *Sex Is a Funny Word: A Book About Bodies, Feelings, and YOU*. Seven Stories Press, 2015. 159 pages. Ages 8–13
Walliams, David. Illustrated by Quentin Blake. *The Boy in the Dress*. Razorbill, 2009. 240 pages. Ages 9–13

For young children
Board books

Biggs, Brian. *Tinyville Town: I'm a Librarian*. 2017. 22 pages. Abrams Appleseed, $7.95 (9781419723223). Grades Pre-K and up.

A town librarian helps a patron find a book.

Blackstone, Stella and Scribens, Sunny. Illustrated by Christiane Engel. *Baby's First Words*. 2017. 30 pages. Barefoot Books, $14.99 (9781782853213). Ages 1–2.

Two dads and their baby spend a busy day together learning new words.

Picture books

Anderson, Airlie. *Neither*. 2018. 40 pages. Little, Brown Books for Young Readers, $16.99 (9780316547697). Grades Pre-K to 2.

In the Land of This and That, where does Neither belong? Neither finds acceptance in The Land of All.

Bundo, Marlon and Twiss, Jill. *A Day in the Life of Marlon Bundo*. 2018. 40 pages. Chronicle Books, $18.99 (9781452173801). Grades K and up.

Marlon Bundo is Bunny of the United States, living a comfy life in the White House. In this political satire for all ages, Marlon and newfound love Wesley work together with their animal friends to vote out The Stink Bug.

Cumming, Alan and Shaffer, Grant. *The Adventures of Honey & Leon*. 2017. 48 pages. Random House Books for Young Readers, $17.99 (9780399557972). Grades Pre-K to 3.

Dogs Honey and Leon have a great life in New York—except that they are left behind when their dads travel. They secretly follow them on their next trip.

Finch, Michelle and Phoenix. *Phoenix Goes to School*. 2018. 40 pages. Jessica Kingsley Publishers, $15.95 (9781785928215). Grades K to 3.

Phoenix is a little worried about her first day of school; what if the other kids call her a boy or don't understand her? Phoenix braves her first day and discovers a warm, accepting environment in the classroom.

Genhart, Michael. *Love is Love*. 2016. 32 pages. Sourcebooks Jabberwocky/Little Pickle Press, $18.99 (9781939775139). Grades Pre-K to 3.

A young narrator with two dads is teased for wearing a t-shirt with a rainbow heart. Colorful illustrations highlight a diverse community, affirming the power of love.

Haack, Daniel and Lewis, Stevie. *Prince & Knight*. 2018. 40 pages. Little Bee Books, $17.99 (9781499805529). Grades Pre-K to 3.

The Prince and the Knight meet when they have to defeat a terrifying dragon, and their friendship blossoms into love.

Jenkins, Steve and Walter, Derek. *The True Adventures of Esther the Wonder Pig.* 2018. 40 pages. Little, Brown Books for Young Readers, $17.99 (9780316554763). Grades Pre-K to 3.

Based on a true story, Esther is just a tiny piglet when her dads adopt her, but she turns out to be less of a mini pig and more of a huge pig. As she grows (and grows and grows), Esther shows her family how easy it is to fall in love.

Loney, Andrea J. Illustrated by Carmen Saldaña. *Bunnybear.* 2017. 32 pages. Albert Whitman, $16.99 (9780807509388). Grades Pre-K to 2.

Bunnybear is a bear who feels like a bunny but doesn't seem to fit in with either the bunnies or the bears. When he meets Grizzlybun, the two help each other find their place in the world.

Love, Jessica. *Julián is a Mermaid.* 2018. 40 pages. Candlewick, $16.99 (9780763690458). Grades Pre-K to 3.

This lushly illustrated picture book tells the story of Julián who, with the help of his abuela, dresses up and joins the Coney Island Mermaid Parade.

Martínez, Ernesto J., Gonzalez, Maya C. and Martínez, Feliciano J. G. *Cuando Amamos Cantamos/When We Love Someone We Sing to Them.* 2018. 39 pages. Reflection Press, $19.95 (9781945289149). Grades K and up.

Andrea asks his father to help him sing a love song for another boy. His father suggests that they create a new song that they can perform together.

O'Leary, Sara. Illustrated by Qin Leng. *A Family is a Family is a Family.* 2016. 32 pages. Groundwood, $17.95 (9781554987948). Grades K to 2.

When a class discusses their families, one child fears that her family will not be accepted.

Pitman, Gayle E. *A Church for All.* 2018. 32 pages. Albert Whitman & Company, $16.99 (978080751179). Grades Pre-K to 3.

Inspired by a real San Francisco church, this story describes a welcoming, inclusive congregation using short rhymes and colorful, diverse illustrations.

Pitman, Gayle E. *Sewing the Rainbow.* 2018. 32 pages. Magination Press, $16.95. (9781433829024). Grades Pre-K to 3.

Growing up, Gilbert Baker loved sewing and design. He left Kansas for the bright colors of San Francisco to pursue his dreams and went on to create an enduring symbol of the LGBTQIAP+ community.

Sanders, Rob. *Pride: The Story of Harvey Milk and the Rainbow Flag.* 2018. 48 pages. Random House Books for Young Readers, $17.99 (9780399555312). Grades 1–3.

As an elected official, Harvey Milk worked with his community in San Francisco to create a symbol for gay rights and continued fighting for equality until his assassination.

Scotto, Thomas. *Jerome By Heart*. 2018. 32 pages. Enchanted Lion Books, $16.95 (9781592702503). Grades Pre-K to 3.

Raphael enjoys his friendship with Jerome: they hold hands, share snacks, and do everything together. Not everyone understands their relationship, but Raphael doesn't mind because he knows how he feels about Jerome.

Middle-grade fiction

Bell, Eric. *Alan Cole Is Not a Coward*. 2017. 272 pages. Katherine Tegen/ HarperCollins, $16.99 (9780062567024). Grades 5–7.

In this darkly funny novel about bullying and troubling family dynamics, Alan is blackmailed by his brother while coming to terms with his sexual identity.

Bigelow, Lisa Jenn. *Drum Roll, Please*. 2018. 320 pages. Harper Collins, $16.99 (9780062791146). Grades 5–8.

Melly hopes that a week at music camp with her best friend Olivia will distract her from the sudden announcement of her parents' divorce. Although disappointed when they're not placed in the same band, they each discover unexpected feelings for their bandmates.

Bunker, Lisa. *Felix Yz*. 2017. 288 pages. Viking, $16.99 (9780425288504). Grades 5–8.

Felix is fused with a fourth dimensional alien and is counting down the days until a potentially fatal experimental surgery to separate them, all the while dealing with his crush on his classmate Hector.

Callender, Kheryn. *Hurricane Child*. 2018. 224 pages. Scholastic Press, $17.99 (9781338129304). Grades 5–8.

Caroline is alone: her mother has disappeared and her only friend is a spirit that no one else can see. Then she falls for new student Kalinda, who helps her track down her mother in the middle of a hurricane.

Dee, Barbara. *Star-Crossed*. 2017. 288 pages. Aladdin, $16.99 (9781481478489). Grades 4–8.

In her middle school's production of *Romeo and Juliet*, Mattie chooses to play Paris because her crush, Gemma, is cast as Juliet.

Donne, Elena Delle. *Elle of the Ball*. 2018. 160 pages. Simon & Schuster Books for Young Readers, $16.99 (9781534412316). Grades 5–8.

Elle loves basketball but she doesn't love the mandatory school dance coming up. She would rather dance with new girl Amanda than with the boys in her class.

Federle, Tim. *Nate Expectations*. 2018. 256 pages. Simon & Schuster Books for Young Readers, $17.99 (9781481404139). Grades 6 and up.

When Nate's Broadway show closes, he is forced to go back to his boring hometown for freshman year. But drama follows Nate wherever he goes, in the form of class projects, musical theater, and a cute boy.

Herring Blake, Ashley. *Ivy Aberdeen's Letter to the World*. 2018. 320 pages. Little, Brown Books for Young Readers, $16.99 (9780316515467). Grades 5–8.

Ivy Aberdeen's house is destroyed by a tornado, leaving her to navigate a crush on a new friend during the turmoil that her family is thrown into as they try to put their lives back together.

Jantha, A. W. *Hocus Pocus and the All New Sequel*. 2018. 528 pages Freeform, $12.99 (9781368020039). Grades 7 and up.

Poppy and her friends, including her crush Isabella, have just reawakened the Sanderson Sisters. (This book begins with a novelization of the original 1993 film.)

Wittlinger, Ellen. *Saturdays with Hitchcock*. 2018. 262 pages. Charlesbridge, $16.99 (9781580897754). Grades 5–8.

Maisie (or "Hitchcock," as she's known to her Uncle Walt) and her best friend Cyrus love seeing old movies on Saturdays. But when new boy Gary starts joining their outings, things change.

Young adult non-fiction

Bongiovanni, Archie and Jimerson, Tristan. *A Quick & Easy Guide to They/Them Pronouns*. 2018. 64 pages. Limerence, $7.99 (9781620104996). Grades 6 and up.

This comic by real-life friends Archie and Tristan offers readers a practical guide about how, when, and why to use gender-neutral pronouns.

Johnson, Maureen, editor. *How I Resist: Activism and Hope for the Next Generation*. 2018. 224 pages. Wednesday Books, $18.99 (9781250168368). Grades 9 and up.

This personal, creative, and deeply hopeful book features words of wisdom and guidance from writers and artists like Alex Gino, Malinda Lo, Jacqueline Woodson, and many more.

MacCarald, Clara. *Beating Bullying at Home and in Your Community*. 2018. 64 pages. Rosen Young Adult, $34.45 (9781508174240). Grades 7 and up.

A straightforward guide that describes the types of bullying LGBTQIAP+ kids face as well as realistic responses.

Klein, Rebecca T. *Transgender Rights and Protections (Transgender Life)*. 2017. 64 pages. Rosen, $34.45 (9781499464603). Grades 7 and up.

This short book provides succinct information on the transgender rights movement and on legal developments in the areas of employment, health care, education, bathrooms, and more.

Mardell, Ashley. *The ABC's of LGBT+*. 2016. 190 pages. Mango Media, $16.95 (9781633534094). Grades 7 and up.

Mardell's self-published reference book is an introductory text that looks at incredibly complex issues from both theoretical and anecdotal perspectives.

Mooney, Carla. *Caitlyn Jenner (Transgender Pioneers)*. 2017. 112 pages. Rosen, $37.10 (9781508171584). Grades 7 and up.

A short biography of Caitlyn Jenner that chronicles her transformation from gold medal athlete to controversial public figure.

Nicholson, Hope, editor. *The Secret Loves of Geeks*. 2018. 136 pages. Dark Horse Comics, $14.99 (9781506704739). Grades 9 and up.

A collection of essays, some illustrated and some not, about love—romantic, fandom, or both.

Slater, Dashka. *The 57 Bus*. 2017. 320 pages. Farrar, Straus, and Giroux, $17.99 (9780374303235). Grades 7–12.

Sasha is an agender white teen living in a middle-class suburban neighborhood of Oakland, California. Richard is a Black teen living in a crime-plagued part of the city. One afternoon, their paths cross on the 57 bus, with disastrous results. Based on a true story, the book is written in a documentary style.

Young adult fiction

Albertalli, Becky. *Leah on the Offbeat*. 2018. 368 pages. Balzer + Bray/HarperCollins, $17.99 (9780062643803). Grades 9 and up.

Leah Burke must navigate first love, her college search, and the unexpected implosion of her once-unshakable friend group. She's also bisexual but she can't find the right way to come out to her friends.

Albertalli, Becky and Silvera, Adam. *What If It's Us*. 2018. 448 pages. HarperTeen, $18.99 (9780062795250). Grades 9 and up.

Arthur wants to find a relationship and Ben wants to get over his ex. After a serendipitous meeting they discover the reality of romance together.

Albertalli, Becky. *The Upside of Unrequited*. 2017. 352 pages. Balzer + Bray/HarperCollins, $17.99 (9780062348708). Grades 9–12.

With same-sex marriage now legalized in the U.S., twins Cassie and Molly's moms are tying the knot. But, as Cassie and Molly each enter into new romantic relationships, the sisters begin to grow apart.

Armentrout, Jennifer L. et al. *Meet Cute*. 2018. 320 pages. HMH Books for Young Readers, $17.99 (9781328604286). Grades 7 and up.

A fun short story collection featuring a variety of romantic relationships.

Benway, Robin. *Far from the Tree*. 2017. 384 pages. HarperTeen, $17.99 (9780062330682). Grades 8–11.

Three siblings, two adopted and one in the foster system, form a tenuous bond while trying to cope with life's many obstacles.

Berube, Amelinda. *The Dark Beneath the Ice*. 2018. 336 pages. Sourcebooks Fire, $17.99 (9781492657071). Grades 9 and up.

Marianne begins to experience scary paranormal phenomena as her parents are undergoing a divorce. After an attempted exorcism with her new friend Rhiannon, Marianne is not sure that she and the people she loves will survive this haunting.

Blake, Ashley Herring. *Girl Made of Stars*. 2018. 304 pages. HMH Books for Young Readers, $17.99 (978-1328778239). Grades 9 and up.

Mara is dealing with a difficult breakup with her ex-girlfriend when her twin brother is accused of rape by one of her best friends. She struggles with her own past trauma and pressure to maintain the status quo.

Booth, Molly. *Nothing Happened*. 2018. 336 pages. Disney Hyperion, $17.99 (9781484753026). Grades 9 and up.

In this retelling of Shakespeare's comedy *Much Ado About Nothing*, camp counselors Bee and Ben snark and flirt while shy Hana and Claudia battle their own insecurities to try to get together.

Brennan, Sarah Rees. *In Other Lands*. 2017. 432 pages. Big Mouth House, $19.95 (9781618731203). Grades 9 and up.

Elliot is recruited to a magical school in a magical land, and works to upend the system's violent ways while navigating relationships with the classmates and creatures of this new place.

Callender, Kheryn. *This is Kind of an Epic Love Story*. 2018. 304 pages. Balzer + Bray/HarperCollins, $17.99 (9780062820228). Grades 10 and up.

Nathan and his ex-girlfriend have remained good friends even after their break-up. Their social group is complicated when Nate's childhood friend (and secret crush) moves back to town.

Cameron, Sophie. *Out of the Blue*. 2018. 272 pages. Roaring Brook Press, $17.99 (9781250149916). Grades 7 and up.

Mysterious beings are falling from the sky to their deaths. When Jaya finds one alive, she enlists new friends to help her keep the being safe.

Capetta, Amy Rose. *Echo After Echo*. 2017. 432 pages. Candlewick, $17.99 (9780763691646). Grades 9 and up.

Zara moves to New York City, where she has the opportunity to play the role she's always coveted. Unfortunately, not everyone is as excited about the production, as cast members begin to die under mysterious circumstances.

Carter, Brooke. *Learning Seventeen*. 2018. 134 pages. Orca, $9.95 (9781459815537). Grades 8 and up.

Jane rebels against the rules of religious reform school, where she is encouraged to suppress her sexuality. Ultimately, she finds love, acceptance, and family reconciliation.

Cherry, Alison, Ribar, Lindsay, and Schusterman, Michelle. *The Pros of Cons*. 2018. 341 pages. Point/Scholastic, $18.99 (9781338151725). Grades 7 and up.

Worlds collide when Phoebe's school band competition, Vanessa's fandom con, and the taxidermy convention Callie is attending with her father are all at the same hotel and convention center.

Cohn, Rachel and Levithan, David. *Sam and Ilsa's Last Hurrah*. 2018. 224 pages. Knopf Books for Young Readers, $17.99 (9780399553844). Grades 7 and up.

Twins Sam and Ilsa throw an intimate dinner party and each invite three guests—but the other does not know who has been invited.

Colbert, Brandy. *Little & Lion*. 2017. 336 pages. Little, Brown, $17.99 (9780316349000). Grades 9–12.

Suzette and her stepbrother navigate their tenuous relationship while also dealing with the fact that they have feelings for the same girl. To make things more complicated, her stepbrother has been diagnosed with bipolar disorder.

Cotugno, Katie. *Top Ten*. 2017. 368 pages. Balzer + Bray/HarperCollins, $17.99 (9780062418302). Grades 9 and up.

On graduation night, best friends Ryan and Gabby look back on the top ten memories of their high school friendships, fights, and romantic attractions.

Coulthurst, Audrey. *Inkmistress*. 2018. 400 pages. Balzer + Bray/HarperCollins, $17.99 (9780062433282). Grades 9 and up.

Asra's power to change fate by writing in her blood sets off a chain of events that puts her in direct opposition to her love, Ina.

Daniels, April. *Nemesis, Book 1: Dreadnought*. 2017. 276 pages. Diversion, $14.99 (9781682300688). Grades 7 and up.

Danny Tozer is a closeted trans girl until she gets the powers of Dreadnought, a legacy superhero. With the powers comes a transformation that can't hide who she really is, much to the dismay of her family.

Daniels, April. *Nemesis, Book 2: Sovereign*. 2017. 314 pages. Diversion, $14.99 (9781682308240). Grades 7 and up.

In Danny's second adventure, she comes head to head with a white supremacist and a Trans-Exclusionary Radical Feminist (TERF).

Dietrich, Cale. *The Love Interest*. 2017. 384 pages. Feiwel and Friends, $17.99 (9781250107138). Grades 9–12.

In an alternate universe where perfect mates are cultivated for their partners, two potential love interests, Dylan and Caden, end up interested in each other.

Dooley, Sarah. *Ashes to Asheville*. 2017. 256 pages. Putnam, $16.99 (9780399165047). Grades 4–7.

Two sisters, separated after the death of one of their mothers, end up together on a road trip to spread her ashes.

Farizan, Sara. *Here to Stay.* 2018. 272 pages. Algonquin Young Readers, $17.95 (9781616207007). Grades 9 and up.

After Iranian-Jordanian Bijan makes a game-winning basket, his new-found fame leads to unwanted attention. When an anonymous picture of him photoshopped to look like a terrorist goes viral, Bijan must figure out how to stand up for what is right—for himself and his friends.

Fine, Sarah. *The Cursed Queen.* 2017. 432 pages. Margaret K. McElderry/Simon & Schuster, $17.99 (9781481441933). Grades 8–12.

Ansa has fought for her place in her tribe, and now she must fight against her own body as magic threatens to take her over.

Floreen, Tim. *Tattoo Atlas.* 2016. 384 pages. Simon & Schuster, $17.99 (9781481432801). Grades 9–12.

In this sci-fi thriller, Rem's scientist mother attempts to cure a sociopathic classmate responsible for the murder of Rem's best friend. But can evil be cured?

Foody, Amanda. *Ace of Shades.* 2018. 416 pages. Harlequin Teen, $19.99 (9781335692290). Grades 9 and up.

Enne searches for her mother in New Reynes, the "City of Sin," using only a name her mother mentioned in her last letter: Levi, a young, charismatic street lord and con artist.

Forman, Gayle. *I Have Lost My Way.* 2018. 272 pages. Viking Books for Young Readers, $18.99 (9780425290774). Grades 9 and up.

Freya, Harun, and Nathaniel have all suffered significant loss. Their lives intersect in New York City one fateful day, and they work together to heal.

Friend, Natasha. *The Other F-Word.* 2017. 336 pages. Farrar, Straus, and Giroux, $17.99 (9780374302344). Grades 9–12.

Hollis and Milo have two things in common: they were both conceived with sperm from the same donor, and they both have two moms. Together they begin a journey that leads them to other half-siblings and walks them through grief, friendship, and the meaning of family.

Gardner, Whitney. *Chaotic Good.* 2018. 256 pages. Knopf Books for Young Readers, $17.99 (9781524720803). Grades 7 and up.

Cameron uses her cosplay talents and her twin brother's wardrobe to pass as a boy so she isn't mocked by the employees at her local comic book shop. When her new alter ego is invited to join their D&D group, she is asked out by Why, who is gay.

Gilbert, Kelly Loy. *Picture Us in the Light.* 2018. 368 pages. Disney Hyperion, $17.99 (9781484726020). Grades 9 and up.

Danny expresses himself through his art. But his art won't make it clear to him why his friend completed suicide, what his parents are hiding, and what's going on with his best friend Harry.

Gonsalves, Florence. *Love and Other Carnivorous Plants*. 2018. 352 pages. Little, Brown, $17.99 (9780316436724). Grades 9 and up.

Danny and her best friend Sara have their lives all planned out. But those plans are derailed when Danny gets into Harvard for pre-med and secretly enters rehab for an eating disorder, where she discovers an attraction to a fellow patient.

Howard, Greg. *Social Intercourse*. 2018. 309 pages. Simon & Schuster, $18.99 (9781481497817). Grades 10 and up.

Beckett, an out and proud high schooler desperate to lose his virginity, and Jaxon, a popular jock with a cute girlfriend, discover their parents are dating and complicate things by falling for each other.

Hutchinson, Shaun David. *At the Edge of the Universe*. 2017. 496 pages. Simon Pulse, $17.99 (9781481449663). Grades 9–12.

Ozzie thinks the universe is slowly shrinking after his boyfriend, Tommy, disappears. Together with his self-destructive classmate Calvin, they investigate the disappearance. Is the universe really shrinking? Or has Ozzie lost his mind?

Hutchinson, Shaun David. *The Apocalypse of Elena Mendoza*. 2018. 448 pages. Simon Pulse, $17.99 (9781481498548). Grades 9 and up.

Elena's mother was a virgin when she was conceived. Now, as a teenager, Elena has healing powers, but every time she uses them other people disappear, and inanimate objects speak to her.

Ius, Dawn. *Lizzie*. 2018. 336 pages. Simon Pulse, $17.99 (9781481490764). Grades 7 and up.

In this imaginative modern retelling of Lizzie Borden's story, Lizzie is shy, never been kissed, and controlled by her parents. When she meets Bridget, the family's new maid, she quickly falls in love.

Jones, Adam Garnet. *Fire Song*. 2018. 232 pages. Annick Press, $18.95 (9781554519781). Grades 9 and up.

Shane's life on the Anishinaabe reserve isn't easy. After the recent suicide of his sister, he finds solace in his secret relationship with David.

Kann, Claire. *Let's Talk About Love*. 2018. 288 pages. Swoon Reads, $16.99 (9781250136121). Grades 9 and up.

Alice is asexual and biromantic, which is something she's been dumped for in the past. She was not expecting to fall head over heels for Takumi, a fellow library employee.

Karcz, Lauren. *The Gallery of Unfinished Girls*. 2017. 352 pages. HarperTeen, $17.99 (9780062467775). Grades 9 and up.

Mercedes Moreno hasn't been able to paint in a year, her abuela is in a coma, and she has an unrequited crush on her best friend, Victoria. Her life takes an unexpected turn when she visits the Red Mangrove Estate: a magical space where art can be created but can never leave.

Khorram, Adib. *Darius the Great is Not Okay.* 2018. 310 pages. Dial Books, $17.99 (9780525552963). Grades 7 and up.

Darius struggles with bullies, depression, and his weight. When he goes to Iran for the first time, Darius makes connections to his Persian heritage and forges a friendship with neighbor Sohrab.

Kisner, Adrienne. *Dear Rachel Maddow.* 2018. 263 pages. Feiwel and Friends, $17.99 (9781250146021). Grades 7 and up.

School doesn't come naturally to Brynn Harper. After her brother's drug-related death, she stops trying. Stuck in remedial courses and considering dropping out to escape an abusive household, Brynn discovers a spark of passion in an unlikely place: school politics.

Konigsberg, Bill. *Honestly Ben.* 2017. 336 pages. Arthur A. Levine, $17.99 (9780545858267). Grades 9–12.

School is tough, and star athlete Ben can't quite figure out what's going on with his sexuality. Is he gay, bi, or "straight with a twist?"

LaCour, Nina. *We Are Okay.* 2017. 240 pages. Dutton, $17.99 (9780525425892). Grades 9–12.

After the sudden loss of her grandfather, Marin moves to college, isolating herself from her past. When her best friend Mabel comes to visit during winter break, she is forced to come face to face with her grief.

Lauren, Christina. *Autoboyography.* 2017. 416 pages. Simon & Schuster, $17.99 (9781481481687). Grades 9–12.

Senior Tanner Scott enrolls in Provo High's infamous Seminar, which tasks students with writing a book in a semester's time. Little does Tanner know that this class will introduce him to Sebastian Brother, a practicing Mormon whose smile ruins him at first sight.

Lawson, Richard. *All We Can Do Is Wait.* 2018. 288 pages. Razorbill, $17.99 (9780448494111). Grades 7 and up.

After a bridge collapses, teens bond in a hospital waiting area while dreading the fates of their loved ones.

Lee, C. B. *Not Your Villain.* 2017. 320 pages. Interlude Press, $16.99 (9781945053252). Grades 7 and up.

Bells is levelling up to superhero—if the bigger heroes don't stand in his way—in this sequel to *Not Your Sidekick.*

Lee, Mackenzi. *The Gentleman's Guide to Vice and Virtue.* 2017. 528 pages. Katherine Tegen/HarperCollins, $17.99. (9780062382801). Grades 9–12.

Henry Montague sets off on his European grand tour with best friend and crush, Percy. The young men embark on a whirlwind journey filled with crime, angst, adventure, and learned secrets.

Lee, Mackenzi. *The Lady's Guide to Petticoats and Piracy.* 2018. 450 pages. Katherine Tegen/HarperCollins, $18.99 (9780062795328). Grades 7 and up.

Felicity Montague wants to become a doctor, but the men of 18th-century Edinburgh and London won't have her. She decides to appeal to her medical hero, but to do so she must reconcile with her childhood best friend, leading to adventures and intrigue across Europe.

Leno, Katrina. *Summer of Salt.* 2018. 256 pages. HarperTeen, $17.99 (9780062493620). Grades 6 and up.

The women in Georgina's family have all inherited a special ability and she worries she has been passed over by the magic as she approaches her 18th birthday. Before she leaves her island home for college, a mystical tragedy about the death of a rare bird rips apart the town and her relationship with her twin sister.

Lo, Malinda. *A Line in the Dark.* 2017. 288 pages. Speak, $17.99 (9780735227439). Grades 9 and up.

Jess has unrequited feelings for her best friend Angie, and struggles with jealousy when Angie starts up a relationship with rich girl Margot. Secrets and violence are hiding under the surface of all their lives.

Lukens, F. T. *The Rules and Regulations for Mediating Myths and Magic.* 2018. 304 pages. Interlude Press, $16.99 (9781945053245). Grades 9 and up.

Bridger needs to pay for college, but the unusual job he finds on Craigslist has him dealing with cranky unicorns, mermaids, and other mysterious creatures. On top of everything else, he must navigate the tricky process of coming out.

Lundin, Britta. *Ship It.* 2018. 384 pages. Freeform, $17.99 (9781368003131). Grades 9 and up.

Claire writes slash fiction based on her favorite TV show, *Demon Heart*, and she's convinced that her ship should go canon. But when she confronts the show's actors and producers at a convention, Claire risks losing everything she cares about, including her new romance with fellow fan, Tess.

Mac, Carrie. *10 Things I Can See from Here.* 2017. 320 pages. Knopf, $17.99 (9780399556258). Grades 9–12.

Maeve is really anxious…all the time! She obsessively imagines the most drastic of scenarios. Just when she thinks things can't get any worse, her mother has to go away for six months, leaving Maeve to go reluctantly live with her alcoholic dad.

Marsh, Sarah Glenn. *Reign of the Fallen.* 2018. 384 pages. Razorbill, $17.99 (9780448494395). Grades 7 and up.

Karthia is ruled by untouchable dead royals, and Odessa, a necromancer, must traverse the land of the dead and uncover the truth when a series of attacks reveal that whole kingdom is in jeopardy.

McGuire, Seanan. *Down Among the Sticks and Bones*. 2017. 192 pages. Tor, $17.99 (9780765392039). Grades 7–12.

This prequel to *Every Heart a Doorway* follows Jack and Jill into their magical world and chronicles the resulting experiences as one sister is apprenticed to a mad scientist, and the other lives a life of quiet, tragic beauty.

McLemore, Anna-Marie. *Wild Beauty*. 2017. 352 pages. Feiwel & Friends, $17.99 (9781250124555). Grades 7 and up.

The Nomeolvides women have lived in La Pradera for generations growing lush magical gardens, but their family is cursed—destined to lose anyone they love too deeply. When Estrella and her cousins realize they are all in love with the same girl, they make offerings to the land in an attempt to save her. The land responds with the appearance of a boy with no memories, whose past holds the key to generations of secrets and lies.

McNamara, Miriam. *The Unbinding of Mary Reade*. 2018. 280 pages. Sky Pony Press, $16.99 (9781510727052). Grades 9 and up.

Mary Reade dresses as a man to sneak into a life of piracy but is stunned when she meets Anne Bonny, a pirate who is not afraid to hide her gender. Mary deals with her gender dysphoria, strong feelings for Anne, and sexual identity as she tries to survive.

Mele, Dana. *People Like Us*. 2018. 384 pages. Putnam, $17.99 (9781524741709). Grades 9 and up.

Running from a secret past, Kay has remade her life at posh Bates Academy. But when a student's body is found in a nearby lake, Kay's tragic past and ruthless methods make her a prime suspect in a murder—and the target of blackmail threatening to expose her past.

Miller, Linsey. *Mask of Shadows*. 2017. 352 pages. Sourcebooks Fire, $17.99 (9781492647492). Grades 9 and up.

Seeking revenge on the nobles responsible for the destruction of their people, genderfluid pickpocket Sal decides to audition for a position on the Queen's Left Hand, Her Majesty's royal assassins. The competition is fierce, and the body count is high.

Miller, Sam J. *The Art of Starving*. 2017. 384 pages. HarperTeen, $17.99 (9780062456717). Grades 9–12.

Matt has an eating disorder. He is also dealing with bullying and developing a crush on classmate Tariq. To make things even more bizarre, he is pretty sure that eating less is giving him supernatural powers.

Mitchell, Saundra. *All Out: The No-Longer-Secret Stories of Queer Teens throughout the Ages.* 2018. 241 pages. Harlequin Teen, $18.99 (9781335470454). Grades 7 and up.

Seventeen short historical fiction stories about queer experiences across many time periods and cultures.

Murphy, Julie. *Ramona Blue.* 2017. 400 pages. Balzer + Bray/HarperCollins, $17.99 (9780062418357). Grades 9–12.

Blue-haired teenager Ramona works odd jobs to help support her family in a town that hasn't quite recovered after Hurricane Katrina. Although she identifies as a lesbian, Ramona is thrown for a loop as she realizes her feelings for Freddie, her male best friend.

Ness, Patrick. *Release.* 2017. 288 pages. Harper Teen, $17.99 (9780062403193). Grades 9 and up.

Adam Thorn is having the most unsettling, difficult day of his life, with relationships fracturing, a harrowing incident at work, and a showdown with his preacher father that changes everything. It's a day of confrontation, running, sex, love, heartbreak, disturbing visions, and maybe even hope.

Ngan, Natasha. *Girls of Paper and Fire.* 2018. 400 pages. JIMMY Patterson Books, $18.99 (9780316561365). Grades 9 and up.

In a fantasy world where there are humans, demons, and human-demons, Lei is forcibly taken to become a concubine to the demon king. She must survive violence and rape with her fellow courtesans, who learn to reclaim themselves and fight for their freedom.

Nijkamp, Marieke. *Before I Let Go.* 2018. 368 pages. Sourcebooks Fire, $17.99 (9781492642282). Grades 9 and up.

Back in her small, strange hometown in Alaska, Corey is determined to find out what really happened to her best friend. But the whole town is pushing her away, which only makes her more determined to seek the truth.

Ormsbee, Kathryn. *Tash Hearts Tolstoy.* 2017. 384 pages. Simon & Schuster, $18.99 (9781481489331). Grades 9–12.

When Tash's webcast based on *Anna Karenina* goes viral, she must balance fame, a frantic filming schedule, sibling rivalry, and deciding whether to come out as a romantic asexual to the boy she likes.

Oseman, Alice. *Radio Silence.* 2017. 496 pages. HarperTeen, $17.99 (9780062335715). Grades 8–12.

At school, Frances is studious and aiming for Cambridge, but at home, she's a quirky artist hooked on her favorite podcast, Universe City. When she is invited to collaborate with its quiet creator, she begins to truly discover herself.

Oshiro, Mark. *Anger is a Gift*. 2018. 464 pages. Tor Teen, $17.99 (9781250167026). Grades 9 and up.

When Moss was a child, his father was shot by the Oakland police. Now, as racial tensions are building in his high school, Moss falls for Javier. When Moss decides he wants to take a stand, he risks losing everything.

Patterson, Kaitlyn Sage. *The Diminished*. 2018. 454 pages. Harlequin Teen, $18.99 (9781335016416). Grades 7 and up.

In a world where babies are born in pairs, Bo is a singleborn, destined for the throne while Vi is "diminished," her twin having died when they were very young. As their lives intersect, they will discover secrets that will change them both.

Philips, L. *Perfect Ten*. 2017. 352 pages. Viking, $17.99 (9780425288115). Grades 8–11.

Two years after Sam broke up with his boyfriend, his dating prospects seem grim. When his best friend Meg, a Wiccan, suggests a love spell, Sam is willing to try anything. But he gets more than he bargained for.

Podos, Rebecca. *Like Water*. 2017. 320 pages. Balzer + Bray/HarperCollins, $17.99 (9780062373373). Grades 9–12.

Vanni's father has Huntington's disease, so there's a chance she will too. In order to be there for her family, she puts off her future to stay in the New Mexico town she's always wanted to leave. But when Vanni meets Leigh, she realizes there are new things to learn even in their sleepy town.

Poston, Ashley. *Heart of Iron*. 2018. 480 pages. Balzer + Bray/HarperCollins, $17.99 (9780062652850). Grades 9 and up.

Ana and her found family of thieves make a living doing whatever jobs they can get when Ana's best friend D09 needs her help. In a desperate bid to save him, she meets a rich, spoiled Ironblood, and together they track down a ship that may have all the answers they need.

Redgate, Riley. *Final Draft*. 2018. 262 pages. Amulet, $17.99 (9781419728723). Grades 9 and up.

Laila loves writing sci-fi stories, but a demanding new creative writing teacher pushes her to work harder and do more. Caught between confusing crushes, a headstrong best friend, and demands of school and family, Laila struggles to figure it all out.

Roehrig, Caleb. *Last Seen Leaving*. 2016. 336 pages. Feiwel and Friends, $17.99 (9781250085634). Grades 9–12.

Flynn's girlfriend, January, has been missing and he is the chief suspect. When January's bloody clothes are found, indicating the possibility of her murder, forensic tests show that she was pregnant. What everyone doesn't know is that

Flynn never consummated his relationship with January because he has been hiding a secret: his sexuality.

Roehrig, Caleb. *White Rabbit*. 2018. 336 pages. Feiwel and Friends, $17.99 (9781250085658). Grades 7 and up.

To save his sister, Rufus has to solve a murder, fast. Unfortunately, his ex-boyfriend decides to come along for the ride, and that's only the first surprise.

Rubin, Julia Lynn. *Burro Hills*. 2018. 244 pages. Diversion Books, $13.99 (9781635761948). Grades 9 and up.

Jack can no longer hide his sexuality when Connor comes to town. But is Connor a bad boy leading him astray or the guy of his dreams?

Rosen, L. C. *Jack of Hearts (and Other Parts)*. 2018. 342 pages. Little, Brown, $17.99 (9780316480536). Grades 10 and up.

Jack is an unabashedly out, sex-positive high school junior living large in New York. When he reluctantly agrees to write a sex advice column for a friend's blog, he also starts receiving "love letters" that become increasingly threatening in tone.

Self, Jeffrey. *A Very, Very Bad Thing*. 2017. 240 pages. Scholastic/Push, $18.99 (9781338118407). Grades 8–12.

Marley has to decide whether it's best to own up to a lie he told or continue to perpetuate it for what might be a greater good.

Shaw, Liane. *Caterpillars Can't Swim*. 2018. 246 pages. Second Story Press, $13.95 (9781772600537). Grades 9 and up.

Ryan, a high school swimmer who uses a wheelchair, rescues Jack from drowning and the two become unlikely friends. Their friendship allows Jack to finally admit he's gay and make strides toward self-acceptance despite the judgments of his community.

Silvera, Adam. *History Is All You Left Me*. 2017. 304 pages. Soho Teen, $18.99 (9781616956929). Grades 9–12.

OCD-afflicted Griffin has just lost his first love, Theo. In an attempt to hold on to every piece of the past, he forges a friendship with Theo's last boyfriend, Jackson. When Jackson begins to exhibit signs of guilt, Griffin suspects he's hiding something, and will stop at nothing to get to the truth.

Silvera, Adam. *They Both Die at the End*. 2017. 384 pages. HarperTeen, $17.99 (9780062457790). Grades 9–12.

Mateo and Rufus both find out that they are going to die today. Over the course of the day, their stories and lives converge. Starting as a search for a final friendship, the boys develop a relationship far deeper than either of them expected.

Sim, Tara. *Chainbreaker.* 2018. 488 pages. Sky Pony Press, $18.99 (9781510706194). Grades 9 and up.

In a reimagined world where time's passing is dependent on the spirits that inhabit clock towers, mechanic Danny is sent to India to investigate a city whose tower was destroyed but time never stopped.

Spalding, Amy. *The Summer of Jordi Perez (And the Best Burger in Los Angeles).* 2018. 284 pages. Sky Pony Press, $16.99 (9780316515467). Grades 8 and up.

Body-positive Abby lands the internship of her dreams with a fashion boutique only to find out she has to share it with classmate Jordi Perez. She has to deal with her growing feelings for Jordi while also competing with her for a coveted paid position.

Spotswood, Jessica. *The Last Summer of the Garrett Girls.* 2018. 368 pages. Sourcebooks Fire, $10.99 (9781492622192). Grades 6 and up.

The Garrett girls have one last summer together in their small town. Oldest sister Des feels left behind, Bea may be changing her mind about her long-time boyfriend, Kat wants her ex back, and Vi has a thing for the girl next door.

Stevens, Courtney. *Dress Codes for Small Towns.* 2017. 352 pages. HarperTeen, $17.99 (9780062398512). Grades 9–12.

Billie McCaffrey—artist, preacher's daughter, and general troublemaker—finds herself in an awkward position when she and her four best friends accidentally burn down a section of their church. The friends, and Billie in particular, find themselves in the spotlight as they work to save the cherished harvest festival and stay out of trouble.

Stone, Nic. *Odd One Out.* 2018. 320 pages. Crown Books for Young Readers, $17.99 (9781101939536). Grades 9–12.

Coop has feelings for his lifelong bestie Jupiter, but knows nothing will ever happen between them because she is a lesbian. When Rae moves to town and joins their tight twosome, all their feelings collide in this messy, realistic story about falling in love, new romance, and friendship.

Sugiura, Misa. *It's Not Like It's a Secret.* 2017. 400 pages. HarperTeen, $17.99 (9780062473417). Grades 9–12.

Sana moves from an all-white Midwest town to California, where she's expected to only be friends with other Asian girls. As she navigates this new culture, she finds herself falling for a Latina girl, and comes to suspect that her father is having an affair.

Surmelis, Angelo. *The Dangerous Art of Blending In.* 2018. 315 pages. Balzer + Bray/ HarperCollins, $17.99 (9780062659002). Grades 9 and up.

Evan returns from summer camp to discover his best friend Henry has become impossibly attractive. As his feelings for Henry grow more intense, Evan's mother becomes more abusive, and he must find the courage to speak up.

Talley, Robin. *Pulp.* 2018. 416 pages. Harlequin Teen, $18.99 (9781335012906). Grades 9 and up.

In the present day, Abby is a high school senior dealing with lingering romantic feelings for her best friend/ex-girlfriend. In 1955, Janet must hide her relationship with her best friend Marie even though she knows there is nothing wrong with their love. Both Abby and Janet find solace in the lesbian pulp novels they read.

Talley, Robin. *As I Descended.* 2016. 384 pages. HarperTeen, $17.99 (9780062409232). Grades 9–12.

In this queer revisioning of *Macbeth*, Maria and Lily are a power couple at their private school. Ghostly accidents start happening after they commune with spirits and madness soon takes over.

Talley, Robin. *Our Own Private Universe.* 2017. 384 pages. HarlequinTeen, $18.99 (9780373211982). Grades 9–12.

Aki is in Mexico on a mission trip with her father's church, and her best friend goads her into flirting with a young woman from another church. Aki thinks it's a fling, but what if it turns out to be more?

Trifonia, Melibia Obono. Translated by Lawrence Schimel. *La Bastarda.* 2018. 120 pages. The Feminist Press at CUNY, $15.95 (9781936932238). Grades 7–12.

Okomo has always been an outsider due to her mother's death and her father's rejection. When she starts spending time with village outcasts, she can no longer hide or deny who she is.

Watts, Julia. *Quiver.* 2018. 300 pages. Three Rooms Press, $15.95 (9781941110669). Grades 7–9.

Libby and Zo come from two very different worlds. Zo is a queer, genderfluid teen from Knoxville and Libby is the eldest of six siblings, living off the grid with her devout Quiverfull family. When Zo's family move next door to Libby, the two slowly become friends, neither expecting how much the friendship will change their lives.

Wilde, Jen. *Queens of Geek.* 2017. 288 pages. Swoon Reads, $10.99 (9781250111395). Grades 7 and up.

Dual narrators Charlie (who is bi and famous) and Taylor (who is anxious and on the autism spectrum) travel from Australia to Los Angeles to attend SupaCon.

Wilde, Jen. *The Brightsiders.* 2018. 304 pages. Swoon Reads, $16.99 (9781250189714). Grades 9 and up.

Emmy King is a teenage rock star and lives like one, until a night out with her bandmates and her girlfriend ends with a car crash documented by the paparazzi. As she recovers from her public humiliation, she comes out as bisexual in front of her fans at a concert and she starts to have feelings for her genderfluid bandmate, Alfie.

Woodfolk, Ashley. *The Beauty That Remains*. 2018. 336 pages. Delacorte Press, $17.99, (9781524715878). Grades 9 and up.

Unexpected catastrophic loss brings together Autumn, Shay, and Logan: Autumn has lost her best friend, Shay has lost her twin sister, and Logan has lost his ex-boyfriend. Told in alternating perspectives, these three unite through a shared love of music.

Graphic novels

Steele, Hamish. *DeadEndia: The Watcher's Test*. 2018. 240 pages. Nobrow, $14.95 (9781910620472). Grades 7 and up.

Barney's folks kicked him out of the house when he came out as transgender. He lands a custodial job at Pollywood, a haunted amusement park named after a famous movie star, where he and his friends deal with demon possession, zombie cowboys, time travelers, and first love.

Black, Holly, et al. *Lumberjanes: Bonus Tracks*. 2018. 128 pages. BOOM! Box, $14.99 (9781684152162). Grades 5 and up.

In this collection of one-shots and specials, the camp friends Lumberjanes embark on stand-alone adventures with magical creatures.

Chii. *The Bride was a Boy*. 2018. 158 pages. Seven Seas, $13.99 (9781626928886). Grades 7 and up.

This memoir shares Chii's process of transition while focusing on her relationship and wedding in Japan.

DiMartino, Michael Dante and Koh, Irene. *Legend of Korra: Turf Wars Part One*. 2017. 80 pages. Dark Horse Books, $9.99 (978150670015). Grades 4–8.

This comic based on the popular television show kicks off with Korra and Asami building their life together in a very changed world.

Ellis, Grace and Beagle, Shae. *Moonstruck, Vol. 1: Magic to Brew*. 2018. 120 pages. Image Comics, $9.99 (9781534304772). Grades 7 and up.

Werewolf barista Julie must team up with her new girlfriend Selena (also a werewolf) and clairvoyant friend Cass to save their bubbly centaur friend, Chet, from the effects of a terrible spell.

Franklin, Tee and St-Onge, Jenn. *Bingo Love*. 2018. 88 pages. Image Comics, $9.99 (9781534307506). Grades 9 and up.

In the 1960s South, teenagers Hazel and Mari meet and fall in love, but they are ultimately forced to part ways. Decades later, they meet again as grandmothers and rekindle their romance.

Grace, Sina and Vitti, Alessandro. *Iceman, Vol. 1: Thawing Out*. 2018. 136 pages. Marvel, $10.87 (9781302908799). Grades 9 and up.

Long-time X-Men member Bobby Drake, also known as Iceman, has always been quick to crack a joke—until a teen version of himself is brought to the future and comes out as gay. Now he has to deal with his sexuality, his family, and his exes.

Grace, Sina and Vitti, Alessandro. *Iceman, Vol. 2: Absolute Zero*. 2018. 112 pages. Marvel, $12.18 (9781302908805). Grades 9 and up.

Bobby Drake, aka Iceman, must contend with Wolverine's son, a new love interest, his old team, and his parents discovering his time-displaced self.

Graley, Sarah. *Kim Reaper Vol. 1: Grim Beginnings*. 2018. 112 pages. Oni Press, $14.99 (9781620104552). Grades 9 and up.

When Becka finally works up the courage to ask out her university classmate, Kim, she has no idea that Kim has a part-time job helping the Grim Reaper.

Kaye, Julia. *Super Late Bloomer: My Early Days in Transition*. 2018. 160 pages. Andrews McMeel Publishing, $14.99 (9781449489625). Grades 9 and up.

Artist Julia Kaye chronicles her transition with charming, light-hearted, three-panel comic strips, originally published as a web series.

Larson, Hope, Ball, Jackie and Hayes, Noah. *Goldie Vance Vol 3*. 2017. 112 pages. BOOM! Box, $10.19 (9781684150533). Grades 6 and up.

Goldie's detective skills are put to the test when she is forced to team up with her rival Sugar Maple to figure out who is sabotaging cars in the big race.

Larson, Hope, Ball, Jackie and Power, Elle. *Goldie Vance Vol 4*. 2018. 112 pages. BOOM! Box, $9.32 (9781684151400). Grades 7 and up.

Mysteries abound leading up to the St. Pascal Rockin' the Beach Music Festival, but Goldie Vance is on the case.

O'Neill, Katie. *The Tea Dragon Society*. 2017. 72 pages. Oni Press, $17.99 (9781620104415). Grades 3–7.

An oversized graphic novel that follows blacksmith-in-training Greta as she joins a group that harvests tea and bonds with dragons.

Rivera, Gabby and Quinones, Joe. *America, Vol 2: Fast and Fuertona*. 2018. 136 pages. Marvel, $12.23 (9781302908829). Grades 7 and up.

America explores her family history and faces off against a new villain in her continuing adventures.

Rivera, Gabby and Quinones, Joe. *America, Vol. 1: The Life and Times of America Chavez*. 2017. 136 pages. Marvel, $17.99 (9781302908812). Grades 7 and up.

America Chavez, Young Avenger and leader of the Ultimates, heads off to Sotomayor University, but in the midst of intimidatingly huge class projects, there are Nazis to punch, entitled cyborgs to deprogram, and creepy fan cults to disband.

Rowell, Rainbow and Anka, Kris. *Runaways, Vol. 1: Find Your Way Home*. 2018. 136 pages. Marvel, $12.23 (9781302908522). Grades 7 and up.

The author of *Fangirl* puts her spin on the new classic Marvel team of teens who discovered their parents were supervillains. Now a few years older, the team has split apart. But when one of their members is back from the dead, maybe it's time for everyone to come back together.

Rowell, Rainbow and Anka, Kris. *Runaways, Vol. 2: Best Friends Forever*. 2018. 136 pages. Marvel, $17.99 (9781302911973). Grades 7 and up.

Karolina's girlfriend comes to visit, and everyone must adjust to life as a team again.

Sell, Chad et al. *Cardboard Kingdom*. 2018. 288 pages. Knopf Books for Young Readers, $9.20 (9781524719388). Grades 4 and up.

Neighborhood kids use their imaginations and a bounty of cardboard to have the most exciting, heroic summer ever.

Tagame, Gengoroh. *My Brother's Husband, Vol. 2*. 2018. 351 pages. Pantheon, $25.95 (9781101871539). Grades 7 and up.

Yaichi, a divorced Japanese father, must face the inherent prejudices of modern Japanese culture and his own feelings when Mike, the Canadian husband of Yaichi's dead brother, comes to stay with Yaichi and his daughter for an extended visit.

Tynion IV, James, and Sygh, Rian. *The Backstagers Vol. 1*. 2017. 112 pages. BOOM! Box, $14.99 (9781608869930). Grades 7–12.

When Jory transfers to an all-boys private school and joins the drama club in an attempt to make new friends, he discovers the mysterious world of the backstage.

Usdin, Carly and Vakueva, Nina. *Heavy Vinyl*. 2018. 112 pages. BOOM! Box, $14.99 (9781684151417). Grades 7 and up.

The new girl at Heavy Vinyl Records, Chris, doesn't know that the manager and other employees double as a crime-battling, patriarchy-busting female fight club. When the lead singer of Chris's favorite band goes missing, the group brings her in to help solve the mystery—and maybe even get the girl. Numbers 1, 2, 3, and 4 of the new comic book series.

Wang, Jen. *The Prince and the Dressmaker*. 2018. 288 pages. First Second, $16.99 (9781626723634). Grades 7 and up.

Prince Sebastian hires talented dressmaker Frances to make gowns for the fabulously fashionable Lady Crystallia, his nighttime alter ego. While Frances loves designing dresses for Sebastian, she isn't sure how long she can keep his secret.

Young, Keezy. *Taproot.* 2017. 128 pages. Lion Forge/Roar, $10.99 (9781941302460). Grades 9–12.

Love story meets ghost story in this graphic novel about Blue, a ghost, and Hamal, one of the few humans who can see him.

About the Author

Photo © Jodi Miller

Named by *The New York Times* and many national and international platforms as the go-to Leading LGBT Expert, both in America and throughout the world, Kryss Shane, MS, MSW, LSW, LMSW (she/her) has over 25 years of experience guiding the world's top leaders in business, education, and community via individual, small group, and full-staff trainings. She is known for making each organization's specific Diversity and Inclusion needs become more manageable, approachable, and actionable in financially realistic ways. This includes physical spaces, hiring practices, policies/procedures, and more.

Kryss earned her Bachelor of Science degree at The Ohio State University in the field of Human Development and Family Sciences, her first Master's degree in the field of Social Work at Barry University, and her second Master's degree in the field of Education, specializing in Curriculum and Instruction at Western Governor's University. She has completed numerous additional training specific to teaching at the collegiate level, specializing in online education from Columbia

University. She is currently working on a doctorate in Educational Leadership, where she continues to focus on how to best educate people about LGBT+ inclusion and affirmation. Kryss holds social work licenses in the states of Ohio and New York, as well as numerous certifications in topics including providing online-specific education, mental healthcare and LGBT+ youth, suicide prevention, and many, many more.

She travels the world working as a consultant, educator, and corporate trainer, as well as appearing at events and conferences as a keynote speaker, an author, and a writer, all of which focus on making schools, businesses, and community leaders more LGBT+ inclusive. In addition, she is currently a teaching associate, lecturer, and liaison at Columbia University and an adjunct professor at Brandman University.

Throughout her career, Kryss has aided in the introduction of Gay Straight Alliances in numerous high schools, participated in the National Equality March in Washington, D.C., rallied for non-discrimination laws in numerous states, and has held or actively participated in meetings with numerous legislators to educate and encourage their participation in the Equality Movement. She has worked in concert with numerous equality-based organizations in a variety of roles to support, affirm, and celebrate the LGBT+ community. It is believed that Kryss is the first person to get a rainbow pride flag included in a country music video; an image of her in front of a rainbow flag and wearing a Harvey Milk t-shirt while participating in the 2009 National Equality March was included in the 2019 lyric video for Trisha Yearwood's "Every Girl in This Town."

Kryss is well-versed in the areas of sexual and gender minorities, including historical and current research. She has significant experience working with transgender youth, transgender military servicemembers, LGBT+ people struggling with suicidality, and others. This provides the foundation she uses to educate and guide professionals to better understand, accept, and communicate about and alongside the LGBT+ community. She continues to actively advocate for LGBT+ rights on the local, state, federal, and international levels.

In addition to being known for her work in the LGBT+ field, she is almost equally known for her lifelong love of tie dye (making her easy to spot in a crowd or at an event) and her never-ending adoration of NYC pizza.

For consulting, speaking, or training requests and for interviews, please visit ThisIsKryss.com.

Index